The Hurley Maker's Son

www.transworldbooks.co.uk
www.transworldireland.ie

The Hurley Maker's Son

A Memoir

Patrick Deeley

Doubleday Ireland

TRANSWORLD IRELAND PUBLISHERS
28 Lower Leeson Street, Dublin 2, Ireland
www.transworldireland.ie

Transworld Ireland is part of the Penguin Random House group of
companies whose addresses can be found at global.penguinrandomhouse.com

Penguin
Random House
UK

First published in the UK and Ireland in 2016
by Doubleday Ireland
an imprint of Transworld Publishers

A CIP catalogue record for this book
is available from the British Library.

ISBN 9781781620335 Hbk
ISBN 9781781620373 Pbk

Typeset in 11/15pt Sabon by Kestrel Data, Exeter, Devon.
Printed and bound by Clays Ltd, Bungay, Suffolk.

Penguin Random House is committed to a sustainable
future for our business, our readers and our planet. This book
is made from Forest Stewardship Council® certified paper.

MIX
Paper from
responsible sources
FSC
www.fsc.org   FSC® C018179

1 3 5 7 9 10 8 6 4 2

In memory of my parents,
Laurence and Mary Deeley

'ARE YOU AFTER LOSING SOMETHING, SON?' AN OLD MAN with a Dublin accent asked, gingerly placing his hand on my arm. 'That's the fourth or fifth time you've gone by me in the last half-hour.'

'I'm just stretching my legs.'

The train's rhythmic clack grew louder in my ears as I stepped into the next carriage, bracing against the side-to-side jostle and relishing the sensation that the ground itself was fleeing from under me. Finally, beginning to feel dizzy, I chose a seat in an empty compartment and pressed my forehead against the cold windowpane. Trees and houses glided past, and bales of hay stacked in high-roofed barns, and plumes of smoke trailing from stubbled cornfields. A low hedge hurried alongside us for a moment, a grey-faced quarry gouged into a distant hill drifted slowly behind. A farmer waved, seeming more to beckon than to greet, and immediately was gone.

The news about my father had come the previous evening, Wednesday, 20 September 1978, while I was out enjoying a walk with my girlfriend, Judy, in Kenilworth

Square. I remember us holding hands as we strolled, and laughing as we swung each other around under the trees, and then arriving back at my bedsit in Terenure to find a message for me left on the hall table. 'Your father has had an accident. Your family wants you to go home.'

I fell in a slight faint on reading the message, and Judy put her arm about my back, steadying me. My father, Larry, had been cutting trees in a place called Moore, near Athlone. This much I knew from the letter he had sent me a week or so previously. But if he was injured, there was no word as to how badly, and nobody I could contact since neither my parents nor their neighbours owned a phone.

Trains and buses to the west had stopped running for the night, so I had no choice but to wait before catching an early-morning train from Heuston Station. Now, bleary-eyed through lack of sleep, I fidgeted, my mind slipping from thought to thought, unable to focus on anything. I leaned back and started rocking, as I had often done on the wooden, unpainted horse my father had made for us when we were children.

Slowly the morning darkened. Rain lashed the window – thin, scar-shaped drops linking and zigzagging into rivulets that trickled slowly down. We crossed the River Shannon with a loud metallic clatter. I peered out at the dim, phantasmagorical fields. They seemed burdened by the sheeting rain, the stone walls and abundant clumps of furze that hemmed them. The River Suck swirled under us as we nudged into Ballinasloe Station. I alighted and crossed the rusty footbridge to where a lone taxi waited as if by prior arrangement.

Soon I was being driven along wet country roads that grew more familiar and discouraging with each passing mile. Aughrim, Cappataggle, little Poppyhill came and went. The rain abated at Mullagh Cross and sunlight dazzled the road. Outside Owenie Connolly's shop I saw two men shaking hands. One of them was my father's brother Mattie. I could tell he was crying. The worst had happened. I knew, yet felt no emotion.

'Will I stop?' the driver asked, as though he had already pieced everything together.

'No. Keep going.'

He dropped me at the head of the little boreen that led to the large, square-faced, two-storey house half-hidden behind the row of cypress trees. I paid him and was aware of nothing more until I stepped into the kitchen where Mary, my mother, sobbed fiercely as she pressed her arms about me. Then my sisters Ena and Bridie, and my brothers Simon and Vincent, joined us on the concrete floor. We huddled together there, holding each other but not speaking. Only after some moments did I realise that the kitchen was full of people. I stared at my old neighbours sitting in complete silence and with slow, scarcely discernible nods they stared back.

It would take days before Simon and Vincent could talk about the accident, their faces still glazed with shock. Neither they, nor my father, had intended going to the wood. There was a field of barley to cut in the small farm of less than thirty acres where my parents kept cattle and sheep and grew some crops. The farm, located roughly midway between Loughrea and Ballinasloe, had ensured that even if money was hard to come by – either from my father's carpentry business or indeed from the land itself – we were at least able to produce much of our own food.

'The barley's overripe,' my mother, the chief farmer in the family, told the others. 'If it's not cut soon, it'll lodge and the crows will swipe it all.'

The morning had started bright but too breezy for felling timber. Then, just as my father and brothers were about to commence the scything, a cloud came over, drenching the barley and causing the wind to die down. So they changed their minds and after speaking with my mother drove to the wood at Moore, about twenty miles from home, where they had bought ash trees for making into hurleys and where they had already been felling for a week or more.

'There's only a day's work left,' my father said. 'We might as well get it finished.'

He vaulted the four-foot perimeter wall – look what the old man was still able to do – but his heart hadn't been in this particular job from the start. The trees at Moore were rooted close to one another and in their reach for light they had grown unusually tall. He and my brothers didn't have much room to manoeuvre. Mishaps came thick and fast that week. The chainsaws gave trouble. It was a struggle to cut the trees, still in their summer sap. One day a falling tree hit the telephone wires at the edge of the wood and knocked them out. On another occasion a tree rebounded so close to Vincent's face that he could feel the draught of air as it kicked past his chin.

He and Simon worked together, in a separate part of the wood to my father – two chainsaws cutting in close proximity to each other would add to the danger.

Towards late afternoon my brothers met up with my father. Now the last of the trees earmarked for felling remained.

'We were gathering to go home and looking forward to watching *How the West Was Won*,' Vincent said.

My father revved his saw and cut low where the trunk widened as it entered the earth. His final tree slid against a standing tree, which kept it awkwardly propped.

'It looks dangerous,' he said. 'I can't leave it like that.'

He cut again, some feet above the ground. He cut right through, raising the chainsaw to near head height – a tactic he had many times warned us against. Maybe he was tired or forgot his own advice, but now he lowered the saw and switched it off. The trunk fell harmlessly away but the upper section of the tree lurched, striking him on the left temple before he could step back. My brothers ran to him. Blood was pouring from his head on to the moss and sawdust where he had fallen. Simon whispered an Act of Contrition in his ear and they could feel his heart hammering fast, then slowing, growing faint.

They shouted and pleaded and ran for help. One flagged down a car on the main road, the other blundered through the wood as far as the forester's house. The telephone wires damaged by the tree they had felled previously hadn't yet been repaired, so there was a delay in making a call to summon the St John Ambulance Brigade from Ballinasloe. They hurried back to be with my father, accompanied by the owner of the wood, Brendan Garvey, who had experience as a nurse. Brendan tried mouth-to-mouth resuscitation.

'He's gone,' he said after several efforts. 'Let him go

now, hard and all as it is for ye. Isn't he better off, an active man like that, than to be laid up unable to lift a finger to help himself?'

The ambulance men and women chatted and laughed freely as they entered the wood. Death seemed no big deal to them. But then they began wrestling my brothers away from the scene. Brendan Garvey conducted them through the wood to his house.

'His wife poured whiskey for us,' Simon told me. 'It tasted no stronger than water in our throats.'

My brothers were brought to the parochial house in Moore where the priest sympathised with them, relating how his own brother had died in the same wood years before – of a heart attack while loading timber. Brendan advised them to leave their car behind and he would drive them home. The parish priest of Moore contacted our parish priest, Father Keane. Shortly after, Father Keane drove to my parents' house. My mother went out to meet him. She saw tears in his eyes.

'Did your husband go to Ballinasloe today?'

'He's in Moore felling timber.'

'I'm sorry to tell you he has had an accident.'

'Oh.'

'Yes, he's in Portiuncula Hospital. I have asked Paddy Joe Hough to take you to see him. He should be here at any moment.'

He said no more, and soon Paddy Joe arrived. He also seemed tearful. My sisters, just home from their day's work in Hohner's harmonica factory in Loughrea, went with my mother in Paddy Joe's car. As they approached Mullagh Cross they saw my brothers coming towards them in the car driven by Brendan Garvey. Both cars stopped.

'Are ye going to the hospital?' Brendan asked.

'We are,' my mother replied.

'Maybe it'd be better to turn back,' Brendan said. 'And say a prayer for Larry at home. He has passed away.'

That's how my mother heard, but otherwise news of the death travelled almost as a rumour at first. It was shaky and uncertain, those who heard it not wanting to believe it or trying to come to terms with the loss of someone they had known all their lives. It still gathered momentum until it was irrefutable on everybody's lips. People from far and near visited our house. They wanted to say how sorry they were and to offer us support.

Provisions had to be bought – chicken, ham, tomatoes, bread, whiskey and Guinness, soft drinks, sherry and port. We ran errands – to local shops in Mullagh, to John Joe Broderick's pub in Kilrickle and to Ryan's at Gurtymadden. Simon did most of the ferrying, his Honda motorcycle droning in and out the boreen at frequent intervals.

Cry, I urged myself, but I couldn't. My father's tallness, his craggy-handsome face, the swept-sideways fringe of grey-black hair, eluded me. Just a few weeks previously we had worked together in Ballydoogan wood and on some evenings while saving hay in the Old Tillage and the Fort Field out beyond the row of cypresses. Then I had gone back to Dublin to resume my teaching job in a primary school in Ballyfermot at the start of the September term and he had written to say thanks and to tell me about the newly purchased trees at Moore. The same flamboyant script as I'd seen him applying to dockets years before in the small back porch room he used as an office. Where was that letter now? Had I thrown it away, the first letter I ever received from him, and the last?

I remembered the night during my childhood when he'd returned from a fair after failing to sell cattle. My mother was in bed, suffering from a headache, and nobody else seemed to be about. I hadn't even thought to light the fire or prepare the dinner.

'All day long,' he said, not looking at me. 'All day standing in the cold, an eight-mile walk to Loughrea and then a three-hour wait in the dark for a truck to bring the cattle home.'

The first and only time I'd seen him so beaten, his hands leaning on the kitchen table and his head lowered. 'There's no earthly sense or reason to anything,' he said, and I felt afraid. It took a good while to persuade him to sit. I kindled the range and threw on a big fry. He became himself again, but that was my first inkling of the vulnerability of my powerful father, though it had taken me until the age of ten to see it.

Not his letter, his day of defeat, his jovial laugh could make me cry. Not even knowing that he would never come home again. I told myself that not being able to cry was normal enough for a person after receiving a shock and that, whether expressed or suppressed, grief wasn't quantifiable. It couldn't be told in teardrops or their lack, or in any outward show. So I denied my grief – but when it did hit, shortly after I returned to Dublin, it came to stay. It replenished, much as clouds do out of rain, or grass following a mowing, or people through sleep. And rather than lessening, it changed, never becoming used up, though the ways in which it would change might no longer be recognisable as grief.

My mother's grief was immediate and fierce. At first she was racked by agony. Then it struck me that she was trying to become utterly 'self less', to spend the grief by devoting all her time and energy to her five children. She cooked and cleaned, chased down 'the thousand jobs'. She talked in between times a breaking rivulet of talk, wrapping and unwrapping her hands about her apron, nurturing and consoling. She gave hospitality to each group of callers, glad of their presence, though they arrived in almost continuous procession and would stay, some of them, late into the night.

Still the grief was there, hour on hour, clutching her. A blotchy tenderness lit the area around her shrunken eyes, a tremble claimed her hands, and the wince on her face would deepen, causing her to turn towards the back porch room where she would cry. Sometimes we'd give in to the urge to go to her. At other times we'd hold back and feel helpless even as we assured each other that crying was what she most needed to do.

As a child I had fought down my giddiness and become the avid listener to whom my mother could express her feelings and reminiscences. In the telling and the listening, we both found something restorative. Now, again, during the brief intervals between callers, she talked and I listened.

'I've no money for the funeral.'

'I'll help pay for it.'

'No, that's not what I mean. There is money, but I can't

lay my hands on it. He told me he'd left it under the loose step in the stairs but it's not there.'

She prayed and then she dreamed.

'I saw him,' she said the next morning. 'He appeared in the dream. But there was . . . a terrible thing wrong.'

She cried and fretted as she told me what had happened in the dream. Again the following night she prayed and finally slept. The dream repeated itself, my father appearing to her – headless – and she awoke in alarm. On the third night the dream came once more but this time my father seemed restored. She awoke with the dream still fresh – it was four o'clock in the morning – and went to the loose wainscot across from her bed and edged it free. There the money lay rolled up and held together with twine.

'His troubles are over and I'm no longer to fret for him. That's what he told me.'

Did my mother's dreams signify anything? They did to her – to the point where she changed, becoming serene in the way she bore her grief. Throughout the more than thirty years still left to her – she was a young fifty-one when he died – she would put on a show of strength for our sakes, but every once in a while she would go to the old back office which wasn't used as an office any more and have a quiet cry.

My father's clothes were returned from the mortuary in a clumsily tied parcel. His personal effects included a pair of dark-rimmed spectacles and an oval, puce-coloured carpenter's pencil. When they opened the parcel, my mother, my brothers and sisters cried again. I felt a terrible constriction in my throat, but still I couldn't cry.

'Stay at this job long enough and it'll kill you,' he'd often said, back through the years, even to my childhood. In the workshop I saw amid the lingering traces of his recent presence a handprint given definition by the sawdust on the metal leaf of the bandsaw. I placed my hand over the outline his had made but it wasn't nearly big enough to cover it.

On the evening before the burial we went to the mortuary. The double doors were shut. People gathered in twos and threes behind us. Eventually there were several hundred present. A subdued mumble ran through the assembled mourners. The fact that my father had died in an accident and that he was widely known on account of his carpentry work helped explain the big attendance. Principally, he was well liked. Some had travelled from Britain and America. They might have met him once or twice, bought a hurley or an article of furniture years before, but they told us now that they wanted to say their goodbyes in person.

His youngest brother, Joe, who until recently had worked as a 'chippie', constructing wooden huts for the use of the workers on the Trans-Alaskan Pipeline, returned from Fairbanks. Despite his film-star appearance – the appealing smile, the navy-blue suit and the mop of black, well-groomed hair – I could see he had a battle to maintain his composure, frowning and unfrowning as each pulse of upset passed through him. Later he would tell us that because life was so sudden and hard physical work a killer, he had decided not to travel back to Alaska.

We waited outside the mortuary for what seemed

hours. When the doors finally opened, a surge came from behind, forcing us forward and to the side. A quick, futile anger gripped me as the gawkers and grabbers began putting their hands into the coffin. I looked around for my mother, sisters and brothers and, failing to find them, began to dig towards my father, scrabbling as through an overcrowded disco or when leaving the stadium after a big match. I elbowed and shunted and felt a fierce, momentary release. Then I could see through a gap in the mill of bodies, see his long pale face at rest amid the light-blue folds of the shroud that was rucked up about it.

The autopsy report would state that a cervical fracture of the vertebrae of the neck had occurred, as well as a brain haemorrhage caused by the head injury. 'The healthiest man I ever examined,' the medical examiner would see fit to say to my family. 'But he's dead.'

Now, as I leaned towards him, a heavy-set, middle-aged woman drew back the shroud to expose a deep, dark wound below and about his left temple. 'What are you doing?' I shouted, reaching to grab the woman's shoulder, but she, seemingly satisfied, tamped the shroud again into place. And though a part of me must have wanted to see the wound, to verify it, I felt I would never forgive her.

Suddenly my mother was there, tears standing in her eyes and all the colour faded from her cheeks as she leaned in whispering to him, one hand placed on the knot of his hands, the other cupping his brow as if to alleviate some headache or fret. My brothers and sisters made their way to the coffin and together we looked on, briefly left alone.

My father was as clean-shaven as I had ever seen him. His fingernails looked immaculate but for a cut on the middle finger of the right hand and the bruised and broken index fingernail on the left. This latter injury fixed my attention. Had he seen the tree falling towards him and tried to ward it off? No, that couldn't be true, for if he had done so, his arm would have been broken. It had happened in an instant and now he was at rest.

The others whispered their goodbyes to him and slowly retreated. I kissed his forehead and covered his hands – wrapped around Rosary beads – with mine. The cold-as-marble feel of his skin gave me a shock. Tears trickled from my eyes but they were automatic, falling saltless on my lips, and I felt little of the anguish I so desperately wanted to convulse and sunder me.

As soon as the priest appeared, a hush fell. We were lined up towards one side of the mortuary, my mother first, siblings then, myself a little apart at the end. Prayers were said and people queued to commiserate with us. Local women clasped my mother by the arm and whispered fiercely in her ear. The men, formal and brief, stood slightly atilt towards her, each with a few all but indistinct words and a watery gaze. I had been away in Dublin for five years and, seemingly uncertain who I was, some even of our neighbours glanced at me before moving off without shaking my hand.

The day of the funeral was gloriously sunny. Somehow that bothered me. We prayed with the priest in our local church at Mullagh, watched on while he sprinkled holy water about my father's coffin. I felt a sudden urge to turn around and there coming towards me was Judy, whom I hadn't been expecting. She held my hand and stood beside me in the packed church. People shuffled unendingly to the front pew to offer their sympathy as they had done at the mortuary.

I helped carry the coffin with my brothers and uncles. It was made of oak and its weight cut into my shoulder. Down the centre aisle we moved, the faces turning to gaze after us and a stumble confounding my every step. Outside the church door two funeral directors came to assist. Together we eased the coffin into the back of the gleaming black hearse.

None of my family spoke on the slow car journey to Killoran, about two miles away. I gaped at the dusty roadside bushes and the dry road itself which was printed with clay marks made by tractor tyres, and felt myself shiver despite the heat. After reaching the small churchyard, we gathered around the freshly dug grave. Three decades of the Rosary were said, the coffin again blessed by the priest before being lowered on ropes by the gravediggers. A fistful of clay trickled from the priest's hand. The green covering was rolled across the mouth of the grave but failed to fully conceal it. The filling-in would take place after we had left.

Some few days later, Simon and Vincent were called to the inquest in a police barracks on the old N6, the Ballinasloe–Athlone road. A sergeant and a Garda questioned them briefly about the circumstances of the accident. Other questions followed.

'Are either of you or anybody else in the family engaged or getting married soon?'

'No.'

'Did your father make a will?'

'No.'

'Did he have life insurance?'

'He did, but it ran out six months ago.'

'The chainsaw looked in poor enough shape. Why was that?'

'Cutting ash timber is hard on a chainsaw.'

At this stage I was back in Dublin. I had returned just two days after the funeral, and Judy, who was a student in University College Dublin at the time, had returned the day before me. I must have thought, insofar as I was capable of straight thinking at all, that my teaching job in Ballyfermot couldn't wait. Our school was very large, with a sizeable teaching staff, and only a few of them seemed to know about my bereavement. I made no mention of the death even to close friends.

'Sir, we heard about your da. We're all very sorry, sir.'

Jason, the smiler – for once unwilling or unable to muster a smile – handed me a Mass card on behalf of the class. I thanked him and the rest of the children and for a moment felt that now, of all times, I was going to cry. Steeling myself, I worked through the hours from bell to joylessly jingling bell. My heart jerked and miskicked; my head burned.

Judy called to collect me after school. We ate at her parents' house and went for a walk. Eventually we took a bus to the Dublin foothills and walked again, negotiating a way between the pine trees. Their needle-leaves wore a bluish sheen, and at our feet hollows held the withered remains of the fallen. We stumbled and steadied each other, pressing past barks whitely streaked with weeping resin, picking our steps around scruffy-looking purple toadstools and weathered outcrops of granite.

Finally we came to a clearing, where patches of ragwort and nettles had begun to wilt. She pointed towards the next stand of trees – at a condom blown up into a balloon and strung from a high branch to resemble a mercury lamp, ghostly and comical in the tremendous calm of evening.

'It's a setting fit for Romeo and Juliet,' I remarked, just for something to say.

'Yeah, but even here they'd need to mind the stingers.'

I laughed for the first time since before my father's death, and then I felt guilty about laughing, but she put her arms around me and said, 'It's good to hear you do that.'

We went back downhill and from a ledge near the foot of the wood saw the silent panorama of Dublin outspread below, blurring through slate-grey haze as far as the horizon. First lights began to glint. We sat and waited until the city was a teeming bowl of lights, pulsing points of orange and white which clustered and sprawled, at once beautiful and daunting as the prospect of the rest of our own lives. The Pigeon House glared infrared. That deep orange cluster, we decided, must be O'Connell Street, and away to the west the trees in the Phoenix Park were still visible, darkly clumped. About us smells of humus and resin swirled, gathering as our field of vision narrowed, and close by a mechanical digger squatted among furze bushes, signifying that here, too, claims would be staked and streets built and peopled and given names. Behind us the trees rustled in a blue-black broodiness of their own, hoarding darkness as if to defy the glimmering streets, their bristly close-packed foliage inhaling and exhaling quietly, sighing – so I imagined – for every living thing.

Back at my flat in Terenure, Judy caressed away my aches and frets as we lay in the narrow lumpy bed. I fell into a dream where I was floating on a raft of moss, the undulant river bearing me slowly, pleasantly, through the wood. Which wood or what river I didn't know. I could hear my father calling me, laughing at my foolishness. I sighed contentedly and stretched my arms and legs out towards the vague edges of the raft, not bothering to answer right then; there would be plenty of chances for talk, we had all the time in the world, my father restored, laughing at my foolishness, calling after me, 'Mind yourself, mind now . . .' I grew aware of the sun, one moment blocked off by leafy overhanging branches, the next poking its whiskers obliquely through canopy spaces. I cupped my eyes. A green luminosity clung between my fingers. Sudden warmth, then coldness, sensations of travelling faster, of rapidly switching shadow and light, of twisting through indescribable pockets of dark into unhindered sunshine only for the smothery dankness to creep over me again. The branches had begun to creak and twist, to stoop and reach. I tried to burrow into the mossy raft but it started to sink, to slowly give way. 'Look out, it's falling. Dad, Dad.' My mouth shaped the words but no sounds came. They had him. They had him now, those pinioning triffid trees . . .

I struggled up through the tangle of sheets and felt Judy's arms about my shoulders, wrestling me awake.

'It was only a nightmare,' I told her, then the realisation of my father's death hit me as if for the first time and I cried bitter tears, with shudders and long-drawn sighs breaking past the catch in my throat to escape.

One night – during the early 1960s, when I was eight or nine – my father told us about the steam engine. 'It was a big gasper of a yoke,' he said. 'Before ever ye came into the world, it made the saw in the sawmill spin.'

He settled back in his chair with his stockinged feet resting on the rail of the newly installed range. The range had Stanley No. 9 printed on it and a temperature clock with a red needle set into its oven door. It looked up-to-the-minute and blockily important, but we missed the open fire's turf coals and dancing flames because they had been fun to look at. Then there was the fact that ours was a draughty house. The weather might be perfectly calm out among the trees and fields, and yet three breezes, one whistling down the stairs and the others sneaking in from either porch, would meet up in our kitchen. Whether open fire or range, we had always squabbled over the breezes, or at least my siblings had. I didn't care about the draughts or the cold – I simply groused in order to win 'the best place'. But tonight the magic words 'steam engine' made us all stop.

'First we thought we'd use a water wheel to drive the sawmill,' my father said, stretching his long legs and resting his hands behind his head after a day making things in the workshop. 'The fast stream that ran beyond near my parents' house could turn a water wheel no bother. It would do you good to see the sand shining up out of that stream bed. My grandmother would let that stream wash the sheets and clothes for her overnight, tied on to a bush with twine. Anyway, we understood that the current mightn't be strong enough to turn the water wheel, in summertime the more so, and we could scratch when it came to sawing the timber.'

He then explained how he got lucky. His Uncle Simeon willed to him the house where we would be born, and the small farm attached to it became his as well. He resolved to build the sawmill near the house and to convert into a carpentry shop the long shed that was used for wintering cattle.

'We bought the steam engine and set it up there outside.'

It was 1938, the start of his furniture and hurley-manufacturing business – and his brothers Mattie, Tommy and Joe helped him. By this stage he had served his apprenticeship of three years at Killeen's workshop in Pallas, cycling uphill each daybreak and earning a shilling once a week for his troubles and a pack of ten Gold Flake cigarettes.

'That steam engine was a thirsty article,' he said, half-laughing and leaning so far back we feared he might overbalance and fall. 'It needed three hundred gallons of water – hot water if you please – to make the piston move. We would fill the firebox with timber and kindle a big blaze. We thought it might be as simple as boiling a kettle. But the best part of the day would be gone by the time the water grew hot enough. Well, that lazy lump of a steam engine dug its heels in for a finish and wouldn't do anything. It just seized up. It was too heavy to shift, so we buried it where it stood and found a more agreeable machine – a tractor – to turn the sawmill wheel.'

Somehow I became hooked to the notion of the steam engine. For a long time I couldn't do a hen's race without thinking about it. I imagined I could go where my father and his brothers had tried to sweet-talk it – as if it was a surly dragon – long before I was born.

'Is it still buried?'

'It hardly drove itself away.'

'What colour was it?'

'Ah, red, I'm nearly certain. What other colour could it be?'

I saw it in many colours. It deepened to the dark blue of the Sliabh Aughty hills before rain. It turned orange or red or garden-shed green. If I was in bad humour, it wore the scabby, burnt-brown look of the exhaust pipe of our Ferguson TVO tractor. And I saw it changing shape, from slim and sleek with spoked and flanged wheels to a big ignorant piece of junk squatting on the ground, chugging and spitting.

And I still hear it, the steam engine that drove the saw, unreliable or rust-eaten beyond recognition or vanished to nothing under the ground. A machine I have never clapped eyes on and yet whose muffled voice carries to me across the years, up through the oil-muddied, tyre-marked hollows left by all the tractors that have stood where it stood, powering the sawmill.

Now when I go back, I lean over the broken ground, the exact spot, and try to get a handle on that lost lazy-bones, the heavy-metal bigness of it. I listen for the hiss of its valves and the pound of its piston. I catch the shouts of my father and my uncles as they scamper and stoop, tumbling logs of wood towards the blur of speed that is the plate saw. I study the means by which my father worked, 'following tractors and shaping timber'. I see my farm-proud mother, fresh as a daisy in her white and yellow dress as she beckons him over to her and gives him some news of house or haggard before taking a gallivant through the wetland meadow we called the Callows, just to get away from the racket. I dream the vaporous progress the old steam engine makes through the blackened sawdust of the past.

My father's face was long and sturdy-boned, with nimble bushy eyebrows, a humped nose and a mouth easily moved to smiles. Once, when I was about two or three years of age, he lifted me up in his arms – a rare occurrence – and carried me outdoors. I pushed my fingers through his thick black hair and tiny specks of fine white sawdust rose, making me cough. He slapped me on the back and laughed. I saw over his shoulder a patch of blue sky and against it the green spires of the cypress trees standing as if spellbound. Through gaps between the trees and then more clearly as we moved over gravelly ground away from the house, I could see the fields with their thick, clay-rampart ditches and feel the breeze against my face, warmer and kinder than a woollen blanket. But mostly I sensed the sun, beaming from a place that was higher than the world, and my eyes told me not to look at it.

Beyond the fertile land, though I could hardly have

noticed it even from my vantage point high against my father's shoulder, lay the Callows. This consisted of a number of large fields criss-crossed by small rivers and divided among a handful of farms, including that of my parents. The rivers, haphazardly linking into each other and some of them meandering as if lost, would overspill their banks usually in autumn and winter, flooding the Callows and propagating an environment where wading birds and rare water-loving plants thrived.

Yes, the Callows formed a little wilderness which, within a short few years, would become my own personal outback, the place where I could lose myself and run free of the inhibitions I often felt while around other people. There I would learn about nature at first hand and feel consoled in the learning. And there, of course, I would shirk the jobs set for me by my parents, especially those that waited in my father's carpentry shop – the very place he was carrying me towards now.

The workshop, which he called 'the shed', had a pale red or purple barn-door entrance and was full of timber. First we got the smells – of must and sawdust – that would still cause my nose to crinkle even after I became used to them. The timber looked naked, flat-boned as if someone had ironed it. We would edge sideways past things. All our visits close into each other the way objects in the distance seem to do. Which is how, even at the beginning, I saw those visits: as objects more than occasions, my father holding my hand, saying, 'Be careful where you step.'

Opposite the workshop door the bandsaw stood, tall almost as the workshop itself. Its blade ran between two spoked wheels, one mounted above the other on a thick black arm that I would eventually come to imagine as the twisting body of a python. When I reached to trace my finger along the dust of the stout metal table, my father pulled me away.

'Don't attempt to go near that ever,' he warned.

I held my hands into my stomach but bit by bit, over several visits, he helped me make the acquaintance of stakes and sheep troughs, as well as handles for spades and forks and rakes and scythes that jutted from slatted grids stacked towards the rafters. If I craned my neck back very far, I could follow the thick electric cables that snaked past the mud-nests made by the swallows before coiling up together in corners. The swallows came and went. They seemed to ignore my father but skimmed close to me as if to scissor-snip my hair as they darted in and out through the always-open double doors. The nests grew bigger, year on year.

Shiny tools and wrenches hung from wall-laths or squatted on the two dusty windowsills. The bench, with stout square-shaped legs and a broad back, was scored with scratches and scars. Here and there chairs and presses stood. Others sat wonkily or lay in bits and pieces. By the back wall blue and orange wheels for horse-carts were spanned with iron hoops, but I also recall segments of wheels that had no paint on them and that still looked as if they could be fitted together.

'Felloes,' my father said, gazing at me, his first-born son.

'Felloes,' I echoed.

He singled out a small hurley from the batch he had left standing against the bench.

'There's a good spring in that,' he said, bending it almost double. 'Here, it's yours now.'

It felt as smooth as silk, for he must have sand-papered it to a shine, but it also felt awkward, too heavy at one end.

'What's it for?'

'It's for hitting a ball – if we had one.'

I swung it at a chip of wood but hit fresh air.

'Lower,' he said.

This time it thwacked the ground, sending a slight shock up my arms. He smiled, but later I would use that 'hurl' to puck a giddy rubber ball in and out the garden path or against the wall of the house, leaving mud prints on the whitewash. Later still I would hit a sliotar, a leather hurling ball, high and hard enough to shatter my fair share of kitchen windows.

In a far corner of the workshop were two large round-shouldered boxes, each with a firm lid on which shone a silvery cross, but my father drew me away from them. A plain door led out beyond the back wall towards the end of the workshop. Several huge disc saws leaned together, grinning and glimmering dully. It was as if they had wheeled themselves through from the adjoining sawmill, for I could pick out their teeth-tracks on the oil-soaked, hardened patch of sawdust.

Day after day he brought me. The bandsaw blade was still, the smell of the timber augmented by the silence, and an air of anticipation seemed to touch every bracket and bolt, every art and part of the workshop.

'Stop here at the door,' he said one morning. 'Just stand and look.'

I did as I was told and he moved in towards the big black box that was yoked on to the shed wall at the right-hand side of the towering bandsaw. Next moment a great yowl split the air, then the spoked wheels spun, scattering sawdust, and I stopped my ears with my fingers for the sound coming now from the pliant looping blade was a tinny, relentless sizzle.

That morning I saw for the first time how the machines ate the timber – they had wodges of it stuck between their teeth – and how they spat out the shavings that curled under the bench and spilled the crumbs of wood that coated every surface. Gradually, over a series of visits, I came to understand that the machines didn't so much eat the timber as chew it into the shapes he wanted before spitting out the leftovers. I wondered at their sharp teeth, just as I wondered at his appetite when he came to the kitchen to gobble the floury potatoes and big forkfuls of yellow-green cabbage and chunks of pale red meat.

One day he put me sitting on the bench and I kicked my legs. He found a torch, clicked it on and passed it to me. Its beam was small and delicate compared to the big yellow sunshine slanting through the open door and the cobwebby windows. I mooched along the bench, towards the sunshine, but he placed an arm around my middle and with his other hand turned the handle of a small gizmo – an emery stone – that was fixed to the bench. Its wheel spun with a hoarse laugh. Gently he placed my hand on the handle but I drew my hand away and this brought a grin to his face.

'It won't bite you,' he said.

He showed me hand planes, chisels, augers, spoke-shaves. I relished the names he put on them but didn't read much else into them or try to determine what they might mean. Still, I could see how fond he was of the workshop and how something was sure to call him back after he had stretched for a while after dinner on the long sturdy bench known as the 'form', with his hands making a pillow behind his head and a snooze opening and closing his nostrils.

While he took short breaks from his work, my mother seemed busy always. And where his hurleys and house-hold furniture, his carts and wheels and farm implements, would find sale throughout Ireland and in small quantities even reach as far as Britain and America, her crafts were the stay-at-home ones of baking and cooking and sewing. Later, much later, the twin-tub would replace hand-wash and mangle. The refrigerator – apart from helping to keep milk and other food items fresh – would largely get rid of the blue mould which she dreaded and which she referred to by its Irish name, *coinleach liath*. The vacuum cleaner would retire the sweeping broom and, as a bonus, rid the house of fleas where even DDT had failed. But while my father's several engines and machines – among them tractors, sawmill, bandsaw and router – delighted and flabbergasted him in seemingly equal measure by virtue of each 'having a mind of its own', she unobtrusively got along with her solitary labour-saving device at this time, a Singer sewing machine.

None of us was allowed to touch the Singer. She prized it as she prized the gold wedding ring that already was tightening on her finger and which, when she mislaid it in her early fifties, would add a small but significant lamentation to the terrible grief brought about by my father's death. The Singer was hers alone, her 'instrument of creativity'. And, unlike my father's mostly old and half-obsolescent machines, it ran with easy efficiency – smooth, she would say, as the cloths she fed to it, the makings of dresses and coats and curtains.

The Singer stood in the light of one of the parlour windows. She worked it mostly on summer evenings. Even then, the parlour – the grandest room in the house, with a black marble fireplace showing off gauzy webs and hazes of pink and grey, a glossy oak table whose legs were shaped to resemble human legs, and a tall oak cabinet whose deep shiny mirrors drank in the pale, embossed wallpaper and the oil paintings of redwood trees and horses – felt cold. We watched the gridded pedal move under her feet and the Singer dance into life. The needle jabbed down-up, down-up, so close to her fingers we fretted as she fed the material in with her right hand before drawing it around behind with her left.

The machine's topmost section made us think of a little horse. There was a wheel where the horse's tail should be and a needle affixed where his head stayed bowed. Sometimes Ena would hold the spools of thread and I'd slip my fingers into the golden thimbles that were full of little dents. I'd click them as loud as castanets until my mother lost her patience and slapped at my hand.

'Stay back while I'm stitching,' she'd say, but the busy machine sounded happy as she leaned close to it, her feet treadling away.

One evening I sneaked new clothing patterns – thin and

see-through and black-lined – from a drawer in the cabinet and ran my hands along them to hear the crinkling sound. A tug-of-war happened with Ena and one pattern got ripped. My mother rose to rebuke us and for a moment I glimpsed our three faces outlined, pale as ghosts, in the window glass before I dodged out of the room.

But of course the kitchen was the place where we – and our mother – spent most time. We constantly got in her way as she followed the rhythms and routines of her work. When my father had completed his afternoon snooze and gone back out to the sawmill or workshop, she'd prepare a cake for baking – flour and buttermilk glugged into dough in a big enamel basin. Always after patting the cake flat she'd use a knife to cut the shape of a cross on its face.

'Why do you do that?' I asked one evening, thinking of the shiny crosses I had seen on the round-shouldered boxes in the workshop.

'So the cake will rise,' she said, easing it off her palms into the oven – a portable metal pot which she had already settled on a nest of smoky turf sods. 'Stay back,' she said, picking up glowing coals with the daddy-long-legs tongs and delicately placing them around the top of the oven lid.

'Why is your face red?' I asked.

'Rosy cheeks are a sign of beauty.'

Another sign of beauty was money. Each Saturday when he got a few spare minutes my father would go into the 'office' and count the week's takings from the carpentry work and then deduct costs. His brothers Tommy and Joe – and Mattie, when he had done some work – would each be given their share. Joe left for America while I was still very young and from then on the profits were shared according to hours put in. With an exaggerated wink, my father would come jigging across the kitchen floor and press his bundle of notes into my mother's hand.

'We'll have to hide it in a safe spot,' she'd say with a smile.

If she happened to be busy doing work about the farm or haggard, he would give the money to Ena, who was the eldest child, a year and a half ahead of me.

'Mind that; it's hard-earned.'

Ena and I often tricked and fooled with the notes. We'd press them to our faces and the smell of sawdust, oil or smoke would tingle our nostrils, but we preferred the 'smell of importance' they seemed to exude when crisp and new. One day we tried to make each other sniff the dried bloodstains we saw on some notes. By the time we had finished handling them, they had become scrunched into a dampish ball which opened as delicately as a rose on the bush beyond the window. My mother would fetch the bundle off the table immediately after coming in.

'Beauty will not boil the pot,' she would say, peeling potatoes or chopping carrots for the dinner. There was a big iron crane above the fire and, as she hung the pot on its hook, she'd assure us that 'when hunger comes in the door, romance goes up the chimney'.

Eventually there would be five children but when there were just two – Ena aged about four and myself that bit younger – we'd kneel side by side at the form, scribbling on brown wrapping paper. I held my crayon in my left hand and she held hers in her right.

'Put the crayon in your other hand,' my mother said, leaning down to show me.

'My right hand fights with the crayon,' I told her. 'Look, it crushes it into the paper.'

'I suppose the left hand is good enough,' she said with a sigh. No doubt she didn't want me to be called *ciotóg*, a derogatory term for a left-handed person, when I started school, but we just worked on, even if our crayons still broke or our pieces of paper developed a hole at the centre.

As we grew hardier my mother spent more time at her outdoor tasks. Across the Callows we'd scan her progress from the south-facing parlour window. She would dwindle almost to a dot, disappear and materialise again, then seem to grow towards us carrying two buckets of water from Keaveney's well. Some evenings she went upstairs with my father and we were forbidden to follow. Or she closed the door to the back porch kitchen and the splash and scrub of clothes against the gridded washing board repeated, repeated in our ears.

'Ah-haaa,' she would say, stepping towards us with frothy soapsuds clinging to her reddened hands after she had twisted the doorknob open. Each time she held out her hands we would scream. Bubbles rising from her fingers would float around the kitchen. We marvelled at their rainbow colours and ran slapping at them as they eluded us or burst damply on our faces.

Uncle Mattie, who lacked the finer skills of carpentry work, being – according to my mother – 'a delay as much as anything', called to our house across the fields via the

old Mass path beyond Hough's haggard once every fortnight. He usually wore a tweed sports coat, a white shirt
and a thin red tie, but always had a slightly crumpled,
stooped look about him.

'If you want something,' he declared in a big voice each
time he bowled into the kitchen, 'give something.'

He invariably wanted a haircut from my father and he
gave us old copies of *Reader's Digest* which we tried to
read. Each time we turned a page, our eyes itched. 'How
can a squiggle have a sound?' I asked my mother when
she sounded out the letters and encouraged me to repeat
them. 'It's all a pretend.'

'The two of us will pretend together,' she said.

One day Mattie brought a giant glossy book called
Flaming Flamingos which took up nearly half the kitchen
table. My mother – who appreciated books, though she
often lacked the money to afford them and though the
library was an inconvenient eight miles away in Loughrea
– said the *Flaming Flamingos* was an improvement on
anything Mattie had brought before, but not exactly
what young children might be expected to get their heads
around, God bless him. I nonetheless fell in love with
this super book even while stumbling over its words and
getting stuck in the mud of its ornithological intent. All
nature seemed contained within its hundreds of leaves –
the Camargue, Lake Nakuru, the Orinoco – as well as
numerous photos of the great pink-feathered wading birds
of mudflat and river basin.

Later, when I walked the Callows with my mother,
the flamingos would light up those river meadows in my
imagination. But now, as I held the great tome open by

pressing on it with my arms, the cover sometimes got stuck to the table's oilcloth and bits of the increasingly dog-eared pages proved edible.

'Flamingos have upside-down beaks,' I told my mother.

'Are you sure?'

'And they have back-to-front feet.'

'Show me where it says that.'

I pointed and she beamed and told me how her mother, Molly Headd, once wrote a ballad that won a prize of ten shillings in *Ireland's Own* and about how, when she herself was a little girl, everybody considered her the best reader in her class at school.

A few years later Ena started in 'baby infants' at Mullagh School, setting off each morning on the mile-long journey with a little satchel on her back and a white ribbon full of brown polka dots dancing in her hair, and returning home each afternoon with both, except that now the ribbon lay flat on top of her head.

'The teacher has a shrine in her classroom with a statue of the Virgin Mary.'

'Isn't she very blessed?' my mother said.

'She has painted conkers and wooden spools tied across the blackboard and we use them for counting.'

'Isn't she very industrious?' my mother said then, her fingertips touching away a stray brown curl that had trouble behaving itself. 'Imagine going to all the bother of picking chestnuts from that tree at the head of the boreen and painting them different colours.'

The teacher – Mrs O'Reilly – lived near us but seemed far away because she was in a bungalow out on the main road. She had silvery permed hair and a sweet, birdy voice.

In springtime she loved to watch the new-born lambs as they frisked and gambolled along the crests and hollows of our ring-fort.

'How soft the wool grew on her,' my mother decided with a laugh, for she had seen what she called the two sides of it, some lambs dying at birth or having to be wrapped in canvas bags and bottle-fed by the fire after their mothers died in a squelch of blood and misery while giving birth. I was let watch the lambing – which my parents termed the 'dropping' – if it happened during the daytime. The mother ewe licked her tottering long-legged lamb and encouraged him in under her to suckle. She stamped her foot at our black sheepdog, Prince, and he always backed off. We would wait for the afterbirth. It dangled from the ewe's behind and fell with a slurping sound on to the mud. We entangled it using briary sticks and slung it as high as we could into the bushes where it flared and dripped – a ghastly parachute.

On fine evenings we joined up with other local children and played in the ring-fort, crushing dandelions on each other's skin and shouting, 'Pissybeds, tonight you're going to piss in the bed,' and suddenly we'd stop when we saw the teacher coming because we just knew she would be mortified by our pissybeds game.

I was six when I started school. The smell of pencil parings and rubbers and headline copies, of books and ink – how far back those smells go, and how long they would be with me, constant companions through all the years of the teaching life I would take up later in Dublin. Smells of schoolbags and lunchboxes, of chalk-dust and wooden pencil cases, of geraniums and floor polish, of damp clothes and sweat, of paint and breath, of holly sprigs withering and balloons crinkling in classroom corners after Christmas – I learned that even happiness had a smell, and so had trepidation. The smells mingled, as did the timber smells in my father's workshop, and some days they came home with me.

Reading stilled and steadied me in a way that nothing else apart from complete exhaustion could. Mrs O'Reilly was kind and it didn't seem to bother her that I wrote using my left hand. One morning a Sixth Class boy tapped on our classroom door and asked that I be sent to the Master's classroom. I thought I was in trouble, for the Master – a tall nervy man with white hair and a deep cleft in his chin – had the reputation of being as cross as a briar. I gaped at the big boys and girls and they stared back. Yet he welcomed me and said he had heard 'wonderful reports' and then he put a textbook in my hand. 'Read it for those *amadáns* and *óinseachs*,' he said, gesturing. 'They are thick as double ditches, the whole lot of them.'

I enjoyed reading aloud but fretted about making mistakes because – I soon noticed – even the smallest hesitation would start a twinge going in the Master's face. But he smiled as I finished the page, and clapped me on the shoulder, and even accompanied me back to praise me to Mrs O'Reilly. Later I noticed a few of the Sixth Class boys glancing in my direction during playtime, and though nobody hit or threatened me, I grew uneasy around them. Still I kept being sent for and, while half-hoping it would stop, coped with it because I understood big words and was able to answer mental arithmetic questions nineteen to the dozen. In common with young children everywhere, I hungered for praise. And, just as the neighbour who's up and about early once or twice becomes acclaimed as an early riser, so the boy who showed aptitude at reading was spoken of as a great scholar.

Though my early success would leave me quite unready when setback and failure eventually fell on top of my head and hard thinking was called for, somewhere there, in early childhood, I became certain that I had been born to do 'a great thing'. This conviction, though founded on nothing but a fanciful notion, would persist – and help me persist – through miserable and unpromising times, right into early adulthood. And what did the great achievement turn out to be? Deep in my heart I suspect there's a small boy still waiting to be 'sent for', to hear word from the powers that determine such matters and might be able to enlighten him.

But during the days of my first school-going, I enjoyed being 'always right' in class and played 'jump the river' with other children as we made our way home with many a meander through the early autumn afternoons. Then there were the blackberries ripe for picking, followed by the apples and finally the winter sloes, and the contests to see who could 'run the fastest' or 'spit the furthest' before a hard frost hit the roadside loughs and changed our game to 'slide the longest'. No sooner had a heavy bout of snow covered the landscape than my father took one of his impulsive frakes and abandoned his workshop in order to help us build a snowman on the front lawn. It was huge enough, we told ourselves, to last for ever. Time passed and the snowman melted and, much more slowly but equally as surely, the gifted scholar turned out to be quite ordinary.

'Go to sleep. It's Tibb's Eve.'

Then not another word, no matter how loudly we called. So we learned to stay silent, but still couldn't sleep. For there were monsters living high up in the dark cavernous spaces above the stairs. At night they would push their rubbery skulls through gaps in the ceiling-boards and peer in at us where we lay in bed. We couldn't see them because they cloaked and hooded themselves with the darkness, but we could hear the creaking of the rafters and sense them dangling, waiting for us to fall asleep.

On frosty winter nights we would itch with the cold, despite the heavy woollen Foxford blankets covering us. We'd clutch the sheets and pray to our guardian angels and, when the idea of the monsters became too huge, we'd pull the blankets fully over our heads. The downstairs voices would reach us, a drib-drab of low mumbles. We'd call out again but my mother wouldn't come running as she had done at the beginning. No matter what fuss we made, she and my father would remain by the fire, talk-ing about the farm and the carpentry work and ignoring us. Gone were the nights when we'd be allowed down to drowse while the glowing coals in the grate collapsed into a nest of feathery ashes.

Still I attuned my ear to catch the voices of my parents. They agreed well together, seldom bickering. There was a clear demarcation: in farm and household my mother

was boss, and in matters concerning the timber my father
made the decisions, though they consulted and confabbed
about most issues. I understood that they both would
always be there. This wasn't to say that they had no
earthly troubles, though generally they kept these hidden
from us. Shortage of money, I saw as I grew older, was a
recurring problem. It got mentioned out loud usually only
in the event of a cow or bullock being drowned in a river
or quagmire in the Callows or dying of blood murrain or
some other ailment. Then they couldn't help but talk in
front of us, their upset clearly less for the dead animal
than for the loss in pounds, shillings and pence. 'Leave it
now,' my father would say eventually. 'There is nothing
that can't be done without.'

Displays of fondness were in short supply in our house.
I scarcely recall a single kiss or hug between any of us. A
gruff word of praise was good enough as far as my father
was concerned, a clap on the back or pat on the shoulder
permissible if somewhat overindulgent, and a brief ruffle
of your hair or a winsome smile conferred my mother's
regard if you proved to be lucky or good.

I developed ways of coping. I would think back
through the day and always what most stayed with me
were images from nature. Sometimes they would flow
one into another, becoming a film of sorts. Poems I wrote
later would work in a similar manner – cinematic currents
grabbing me up, getting me there. So the frost patterning
the bedroom window would clear and I would be able
to see right into the workshop where earlier I might have
found a wingless wasp asleep on a chunk of wood. The
wasp would awake and sprout new wings and fly out of

the workshop, landing on one of the wooden posts of my mother's clothesline. It would nibble at the weather-bleached post and I'd hear the distinct scrape of its teeth and see perfectly clearly the small clean patch of fresh wood it was opening under the old. The images would turn and return, and bring restfulness.

Whoooooosssshh!

The breeze would fill the row of cypresses with sighs. I would slip into a dream because the bed was a magic carpet lifting me through the immaterial slates and rafters, out and over the darkened fields, the bushes and rooftops. On such flights I never felt cold, but pleasant sights could instantly give way to troubling ones – the freshly skinned lamb, blue-veined and glistening, that hung from Paddy Joe Hough's door, the scruffy bundle of rats I'd seen squabbling on the main road, the hawk that sometimes hovered in ever-dwindling circles above our haggard while the hens ran for cover and the pig looked up from his rooting and grunted in a voice I had never heard from him before.

And suddenly the monsters would be back.

I felt sorry for I was the one who had told my brothers and sisters about them in the first instance and now they found it difficult to sleep. Eventually my father, dressed in his long johns, would come to say goodnight and pull the door behind him at my request. It would scrape against the floor and never fully close. Still, his presence, however brief, seemed to break the monsters' spell. Slowly they shrivelled and faded. We learned to laugh at them and called them mugginses.

In time I grew to love the darkness for its mystery and

potential. I would listen to the sound of the vixen barking in the Callows at night.

Wheeeu! Wheeeu!

Her shrieking made it seem as if she was pleading for the company of other foxes. But when she uttered a single bark, all the dogs, including our own, would woof rowdily from their respective yards and then she wouldn't bark any more because she would know where they were. I would fall asleep and dream of her – stealthily pushing through the undergrowth, plotting her next move.

Some nights, however, a sudden sadness would touch me right in the place where my heart was and I'd put my hand there and feel the steady thump, and wonder what dying meant. I'd seen animals that had died being buried in bog holes or ditches and I worried that the same might happen to me and wondered whether it would be soon, though I knew without even having to think about it that my parents were immortal and couldn't die and I consoled myself that they would have no choice but to feel sorry for me in the end. The sadness would slip away, often into dreams of falling – freely and pleasurably – off trees, into wells, out of the very dreams themselves. The most vivid of my dreams blended naturally into what I assumed any practical, no-nonsense person would agree was real.

One morning while the house still slept, I stole out to the landing window for I had heard a strange loud fluttering noise. The window was full of tortoiseshell butterflies. They skittered and bashed themselves against the glass as the sunlight streamed in, highlighting the yellow and dark amber of their black-marked wings, the blue-spotted fringes. They quivered and flapped. Then I saw other tortoiseshells flickering in ones and twos from the dark spaces above the stairs to join them at the window. They had been hibernating in the recesses where we had imagined the monsters to exist. Now the sunshine and the first warmth of the year called to them. I opened the window's upper section by removing the leg of wood that kept it propped in place – the sash cord was broken – and away they scattered to the fresh outdoors. I felt full of goodness. It was the beginning of spring.

'Be kind to your mother,' my father would say. 'Ye aren't able to understand yet what she has to go through.'

More and more she was taking 'rests'. She would suddenly flop out of breath on to a chair, unable to do much housework or farming now, or to fetch water from the well. But even while sitting by the fire she kept herself busy, polishing and mending, knitting woolly jumpers based on the styles she found in *Woman's Way*.

Mrs Heagney, our next-door neighbour, who earned her living as a dress-maker, would help around the house. Her frail appearance – accentuated by a lame step and the pallor of her face on which sat small thin-rimmed glasses – concealed her resourcefulness. It seemed as if she could make clothes out of nothing, and when she wasn't dress-making she earned what she called 'pin money' by dusting the church and the school twice a week.

Mrs Hough, our other near neighbour, who wore her hair in a bun and had a habit of pursing her lips and running her tongue around inside her mouth, also visited my mother. Her face was firm-boned and beautiful, even if lined with many small wrinkles. She enjoyed smoking cigarettes and her quick wit and irreverent laugh made her sound younger than her years. She knew the skills of midwifery and was also called on when it came to the laying out of the dead.

She would say 'I smell greens' each time she came in, even if there weren't any vegetables being cooked. Maybe she could pick up the lingering smell of my father's over-boiled cabbage for, as my mother rested, he turned his hand to cooking and cleaning. Our dinners no longer tasted as good.

'Wait till I tell the other men,' Mrs Hough would tease him, 'how you're after making a holy show out of them.'

'I won't bake bread,' he'd say back. 'That's one job I won't do.'

Instead, he bought a white loaf at Owenie Connolly's shop that, though it had a delicious crust and a fresh, airy taste, left us feeling hungry nearly as soon as we'd eaten it.

When the housework was completed, he would take us for jaunts on the donkey's back. He also kept a jennet, but declared that it was 'about as much use as an ornament bought at the October Fair in Ballinasloe'. On one jaunt he gave the donkey's rump a slap, quickening it, and we began to slide off. He caught us at the last moment and set us upright. This started a scary game that turned into many a laugh. We grew casual, and so did he. And when he left it too late to catch us, we fell into a muddy Callows drain. My mother noticed our wet and dirty clothes and read him his three generations.

'Are you trying to drown my children?' she asked.

'No, I'm trying to make them independent.'

The jaunts on the donkey stopped, but we still got out of doors, tramping across the fields to our grandmother Bridget Deeley's house, where our aunts and uncles also lived. We took turns on my father's shoulders now, and whoever had to walk couldn't get bored because there was the constant swish of the grass whispering secrets. 'Make sure to shake hands with your grandmother because she is a very important person, and say, "How are you, ma'am?"'

The branches of an apple orchard overleaned the big wrought-iron gate, and there she stood looking old and dainty and a little lost in the wide cobblestone yard of her half-thatched, half-slated house. She wore gold earrings and her hair was gathered in a net. We followed her to the kitchen where she took a bar of chocolate from the mantel and broke it between us before wetting the tea for my father. I remember feeling vexed with him on the trek home because he had insisted we give back the florins she had lined our palms with.

About that time also there were the Callows walks where he forgot, if only for the time being, the demands of housework and carpentry shop, and brought us through thickets of wild flowers and squelching wetland. Our play became his play, with a whiff of danger in our nostrils and the start of wonderment in and behind the eyes which – when I was older – would have me forgetting the world of people and the give-and-take between them as I wandered the Callows on my own.

A pronounced dip happened where the Callows began,

at the end of the field known as Old Tillage, and this dip stretched over several loosely fenced fields. The first river, running east, blocked our path. It was guarded by a clayey moot topped with a few perished grey stakes and some stray strands of thorny wire. My father would carry us, one at a time, across. The second river, known as the 'middle' river, had high banks and ran south, accompanying us. Water flowed dark and secretive under its two narrow stone bridges. At the third river, which flowed fast and wide, combing long tendrils of grass with its current, he would gather one of us in his arms and take a running jump. Then he would jump back in order to transfer the next child. It thrilled us, that sensation of being whizzed across while yet cradled by my father, and before long he found himself pestered as all of us wanted not just to go across but back again, across and back, several times.

The squelches grew louder, the ground more thin-skinned. A swallow-hole would bubble and fart and we'd laugh. At the very centre a whirlpool twisted and flexed – so full of commotion you could see neither sky nor clouds reflected there. Nothing grew in that mud-bath and we had to promise to always stay away from it.

'Flaggards,' my father said as we waded through tall clusters of wild irises unpeeling purple and yellow blossoms at the end of our part of the Callows.

'Flaggards,' we chorused back.

Birds would shoot upwards with explosive wing-beats that startled us, and once I twisted my ankle on a clump of rushes after a hare sprang in a broad sideways arc just as I was about to step on him.

Flowers of different kinds floated or stood knee-deep in pools or embroidered themselves around the water's edge. Our feet stirred up spiders and frogs, moths and dragon-flies. We saw butterflies – several of them small and pale blue, others large and, according to my father, capable of frightening a bird away with one flap of their intensely coloured wings. Finally we would look back, amazed at how far behind we had left our house.

Keaveney's well rose out of the last, biggest river. A concrete surround prevented cattle from soiling it. I would step over the shaky stones, battling a reel in my head. The well swirled as if being stirred by an invisible stick. There was no end to the water. It kept escaping through a hole in the side of the surround and splashing and spreading, yet for all that, Keaveney's well never got any smaller.

My mother seemed to grow more tired the more she rested.

'Keep the noise down,' my father would whisper, tip-toeing around her.

Eventually Mrs Hough and Mrs Heagney would arrive together, and the whole house would quicken into a hurry.

'You're staying with Mrs Heagney for a few days.'

'Why are we staying?'

'You're staying for a holiday.'

Mrs Heagney, accompanied by her daughter, who was about the same age as Ena, would walk us the short distance to her house, and Mrs Hough would remain with my mother.

'Where did you get the lame step, Mrs Heagney?' I would ask.

'Oh, I was born with a dislocated hip.'

'Why don't you fix it?'

'It could have been fixed when I was a child, but back then people seldom bothered to change the things you were born with and now it can't be helped.'

'Are you sorry so?'

'No indeed. I'm still able to ride a bicycle.'

She gave us open-air baths under the old Sitka spruce trees where we would dance and splash in the galvanised tub before being sent early to bed. On our last 'stop-over', we were let watch while she worked in her dress-making parlour. 'This is a parcel a neighbour received from America,' she told us. Inside was a fancy coat with orange buttons.

'Well now,' she said, ripping the seams and scissoring off the buttons, 'that won't suit the Irish weather at all – it's too flamboyant.'

Briskly, her long-practised hands turned the material inside out and fashioned a new, sober-looking coat and found a set of grey buttons to go with it.

There were two of us on the first 'holiday', three on the second, and four on the third. Our holidays always ended with Mrs Heagney walking us home. Each time we'd return to a house full of whispers. My mother's sister Freda and other relations would be there, as well as some neighbours – Mrs Hough, Mrs Shiel and Mrs Maguire. We'd have to promise to stay so quiet that we wouldn't be heard behind a newspaper and my father would nudge us into the parlour. There my mother would sit propped by her pillow in a bed draped with white eiderdown. Cradled in her arms we'd see the surprise that each and every time came as a surprise – a new baby.

Mick Dillon opened the half-door of his thatched cottage and welcomed us in. He was old with a complexion of greyish white as if he had never ambled far from the low winter light of his kitchen. 'It's a lonely spot,' he said, pulling up chairs for us and clearing a space at the table. 'Still and all, it's the exact centre of the universe.'

'People say he's strange because he doesn't go to Mass,' my father had explained on the long walk to the far reaches of Foxhall Little. 'But he has his own mind, and who's to know if he's right or wrong anyway?'

There were signs of his strangeness everywhere. Mountains of newspapers piled in corners; a lidless teapot left to brew under a kettle; a few hens roosting on a sooty, pivoting iron crane above the hearth; an orange cat curled up nursing her kittens in a straw basket on top of the dresser.

'Amn't I lucky all the same,' he crooned, his voice full of quavering wonder and excitement as he corralled and conducted the space in front of him with his arms. 'Wouldn't it be worse if I lived out by the side of the Lurgan road? If you ventured too far in that direction, beyond the bog and the mist, you might fall off the face of the Earth altogether and find yourself landed among the stars.'

He moved to the dresser and poured a bottle of white lemonade into cups for us to drink. 'Do ye believe in ghosts?' he asked, grinning and regarding us intently. 'I would never stir out from the house after duskus because day is for the living and night is for the dead.'

His laugh didn't stop our eyes from goggling.

'Would you ever consider getting the electricity installed?' my father asked after buying hay off him and partaking of 'a tincture' from a cracked mug.

'No,' he said. 'Isn't the juice more dangerous than the ghosts? Didn't I witness it above in Gurtymadden, one live wire sparking and thumping against a damp wall?'

'You did,' my father agreed. 'But people find the electricity a great convenience all the same.'

'I wouldn't have it,' Mick asserted in a loud, hoarse burst. 'There's a boundary, you know. There's nature and there's super-nature. Where nature stops and where super-nature commences is never fully determined. It'll be a sad day for the world when scientists and such are able to draw a line putting nature here and putting super-nature nowhere.'

Mick Dillon wasn't the only believer in this 'boundary between two worlds'. Not many years had passed since the parishioners stood gathered while a man fixed a bulb to a pole in Gurtymadden – or was it at Mullagh Cross? Until then they had considered night a separate element, with only oil lamps to stand against the dark of winter. Ghosts bloomed in their imaginations. They told each other stories before retreating to bed in observance of the clear divide between day and night.

I have a vague memory of the outline of a paraffin lamp impressed on our kitchen wallpaper, that part of the wild dog rose pattern still looking new and fresh where the area about it had become suntanned. And a clearer memory of discarded lamps, thrown under the bench in the workshop where they gathered dust and were inhabited by spiders. But all I am certain about is that, when the bulb on the pole was lit, my parents in common with most local people jumped at the chance to install the magical new electrical power.

Tar-treated poles were planted heel first and pushed upright. Wooden cable spools were rolled along after the poles and the cables yoked up to link house to house through the remote countryside by men who climbed the poles using a special harness and spiky boots. I could perfectly understand why people would take turns to switch the light on, off, on, or hurry outside to marvel at the brightness in their windows. Electricity became their way of banishing old ghosts, but schooling would begin to uncover for us the secrets of electricity – and much else besides, including the mysteries of night, the place that Mick Dillon had said belonged to the dead.

'First,' the Master instructed – I was in Fifth Class at this stage – 'close your eyes and think of the dark night covering everything except when the moon shines and the stars are out. Now think of someone, or maybe a straggle of people, burning a hole in the darkness by rubbing two sticks together and kindling a bit of dry vegetation and carrying fire around with them.'

That, we were told, was the start of all our ingenious ways of seeing in the dark. Imagine, the Master said, and imagining came easily to me. I closed my eyes and imagined a rush-light dithering in a cave, a candle flickering on my mother's sideboard, a paraffin lamp nailed up in the carpentry shop with a glass mantle that glowed. For a finish I pictured my parents carrying battery lamps with their beams of light arcing and springing across frosted grass in the middle of the night because the sheep were lambing.

Rural electrification, the Master said, was called 'the quiet revolution'. And when he asked the class about the uses of electricity, I thought of the fridge my mother would love to buy, the washing machine and the vacuum cleaner she had in mind, and I knew she would say 'the quiet revolution' had a fair bit to travel yet. I thought of the television set that only Vincie Lyons seemed able to afford, and how we would crowd into his shop each third Sunday in September to watch Galway win another football All-Ireland. I heard the howl of our bandsaw when you started it, and saw the yellow signs with the zigzag of red painted-on lightning on the electricity poles themselves and on the wall beside the bandsaw motor that warned 'Danger! Keep away; it is dangerous to touch the electric wires.'

Throughout my two years in his classroom the Master pushed us hard. He didn't spare himself, but neither did he spare anybody who had difficulty in keeping up. Still, with each question he asked, a bustle of excitement would take hold in my chest and I would raise my hand and, often as not, he would pick me and the answer would be right. The satisfaction of being right seldom could match the anticipation of answering, however. And I suspect I would have ditched all the easy school praise for a few words of approval thrown sideways at home. Such praise was rare and precious. You had to prove yourself 'useful' to earn it. You had to be practical, show yourself able to make and do, help in the routine struggle of farm and carpentry work – but I felt increasingly at odds with everything, not least with myself. I flew into tantrums and exasperated my parents' hearts.

But that happened later. At first the natural world in its shimmering grandeur seemed to approve and encourage me as a dreamer. One night when I was about six or seven I saw a strange, sprightly light shining on the bedroom door. It looked bluish white and seemed to come obliquely through the window from the direction of the Callows. I didn't feel afraid as I watched it move – playfully almost – up and down the door as if being thrown and caught by an unseen hand. I must have watched for an hour or more before drifting off to sleep. I lay awake the following night in the hope of seeing it again, but it didn't show. Many nights were to pass until – just when I had convinced myself it was never really there – it shone lively and haunting as before.

'Are there ghosts?' I asked my mother.

'I've never seen a ghost,' she said.

'Day is for the living,' my father said, echoing Mick Dillon, 'and night is for the dead.'

I told them about the light and my mother said maybe it's what some people call will-o'-the-wisp, others Jack the Lantern. 'He's supposed to be an evil spirit who leads people astray at night into dangerous places such as swamps and rivers, and he carries a little lamp.'

Seeing the look on my face, she immediately retracted. 'It's all nonsense. The day will come when someone will prove that even if there is a light, there's a good explanation behind it.'

'There is a light,' my father asserted. 'Haven't I seen it myself wandering the Callows? It would move away if you tried to catch it, or it might swing around behind you if you turned your back.'

'You'll upset the child,' my mother said. 'It's only a natural flame coming out of the ground.'

'And what causes it to move? Why doesn't it leave burn-marks after it if it's only a natural flame?'

'I wouldn't bother my head with it,' she said. 'It does no good thinking about some things.'

'Well, that light did me a power of good one night,' my father said. 'I was sixteen years of age. Old enough to know it saved me when I was running home to my parents' house beyond after a game of cards at O'Donnell's of Finnure. The night was pitch dark and I was heading straight for the swallyhole when the light sprung up in front of me and I saw a shine on the water.'

Several times I would see will-o'-the-wisp reflected on the bedroom door over the following years, and on one occasion it danced while I stood at a distance in the Callows. It held me far more than the idea of Christmas presents or Santa Claus ever did. It fired my imagination in ways the workaday world never could. Long after the distancing that books and formal education helped to bring, I would still feel wistful at the memory of it. And then I found it again – in literature, ranging from Milton's *Paradise Lost* to Coleridge's *The Rime of the Ancient Mariner*:

> About, about, in reel and rout
> The death-fires danced at night;
> The water, like a witch's oils,
> Burnt green, and blue, and white.

Eventually it would become reduced, more or less, to methane gas, though not completely explained away. With it would pass other wonders I witnessed as a child, not least the *seoidín na mara* – the 'jewels of the sea' – which brought a starry shimmer to our skin, and the ghost wind that on perfectly calm summer days could swirl the hay we were saving into a little twister of its own.

I found myself writing poems about will-o'-the-wisp, and now, even if the poems themselves and the not always merry dance they lead me might vanish into thin air, I still nod my head in agreement with Emily Dickinson's words:

> Better an ignis fatuus
> Than no illume at all.

One morning when I was about nine, the fire wouldn't catch. My mother had followed her usual routine, lighting a bundle of shavings around which woodchips and sods of turf were stooked, but after the initial blaze-up the fire refused to take. The chimney sent buckling billows of smoke back to hang about the mantelpiece. The black grate looked surly now, and so did my mother.

'It's those blasted jackdaws,' she said, getting heavily to her feet and letting the fire shovel clatter from her hands.

'Are you sure it's the jackdaws?' my father asked.

'Why,' she said, 'am I expected to do everything? Ye all think so much of bothering to arrive down for your breakfasts – do I have to eat the food as well?'

And then she said mightn't the best way to make sure about the blocked chimney be for someone to go up on top of the roof and find out?

He didn't answer but he walked out to the shed and

we traipsed behind him. He lifted the sturdy pinewood ladder and placed it against the house. It reached only as far as the eave chutes, so he got the much lighter slating ladder and climbed with it slung across his shoulder up the big ladder towards the eaves. We stood staring after, against the sunlight and the thin blue air, while my mother – overcoming her annoyance – held the foot of the big ladder for fear it might slip.

When my father neared the top, he placed the slating ladder along the incline of the roof and climbed again until he had reached the chimney stack. We could see him there, hugging the house, delving his arm as far as the oxter down into the chimney, vigorously rooting until his head and shoulders had all but disappeared.

'Maybe he'll find an echo,' I joked, thinking of the echo in Hough's chimney whose clean, high voice always sounded back across the fields to us when we shouted 'Toby', the name we'd chosen for it after coming to regard it almost as a living presence.

'There's no echo to find,' my mother said. 'That's foolish talk.'

Suddenly a nest of twigs rolled rattling down the slates. Then my father tossed down tufts of moss, together with more loose sticks and a faded red cardigan that the jackdaws must have pilfered from the clothesline. He stooped to bowl an egg towards us but it gathered pace and did a little bounce that took it past the eaves and it broke at our feet, leaving an orange smear and fragments of pale-blue shell that had blackish markings all over them.

When I looked up again, he was standing on the wide

chimney wall. He began to dance, clip-click, clip-click, a hobnailed quickstep. He waved his hands about. He clasped them on top of his head. I saw the grin plastered across his face as he danced. I always loved the entertainments he put on for us. They happened but seldom and never seemed planned, and now there he was, putting on another one. Somehow, in separating him from his work, his high jinks helped free me from any expectations he might have of me as well.

'What's he up to?' my mother wondered, trying to crane her neck while she stood minding the ladder.

'He's dancing.'

'Come down out of that!' she shouted, stepping away and waving the goose-wing duster she had taken from the fireplace. 'You're frightening the children.'

Now all of us shouted, but our pleadings didn't seem to be tall enough. He kept on dancing. In fact, he laughed and then danced all the faster. 'I'll come down,' he shouted to my mother, 'as soon as you tell me you love me!'

'Love' was a word our family just didn't use, ever. Hearing my father use it now was even stranger to me than the fact that he had chosen to dance on top of the chimney stack before saying it. My mother flinched as if she'd been hit. 'He's cracked as a bottle,' she said, and again shouted for him to come down. 'Has he no shame? Why is he upsetting everyone?'

It dawned on me that he was dancing for her, not for us. He was playing a game, except parents weren't supposed to play games, never mind risky games, with each other. All he did was to ask again, as insistent now as Toby's echo and loud enough for Hough's house and Heagney's house and Mrs O'Reilly's house and maybe every one of the neighbours' houses to hear. He wouldn't quit, and we turned towards my mother, asking her to please make him stop.

'I do,' she said in a quiet, defeated way at last. And when he still asked, she said 'I do' more loudly and he stopped.

If she had waited a moment longer she might have won the game, for suddenly smoke rose in a crooked coxcomb from the chimney, causing my father to crouch away from it on to the slating ladder and begin his descent. We all clutched the pinewood ladder to make sure it was solid, but my mother's face was wreathed in redness.

The fright is over, we agreed; he's coming down. But as he stepped on to the top rung of the heavy ladder, his foot slipped and after a brief wrestle he lost his balance. I saw his arm flail and still he was falling, in what I can only describe as slow motion, though there was no time for us to shout out or do anything other than gape. Then an amazing thing happened. He swung his hand on to the metal pipe that angled out from the wall, and his grip held long enough for the pipe to break his fall so he was able to twist acrobatically, avoiding the water barrel and landing in front of us with a clang of his hobnailed boots.

My mother looked bewildered, even lost. She clutched his arm against her stomach and chest. 'You're a very foolish man,' she said, and he looked at her and seemed to agree. Our parents never kissed or embraced in front of us because – as my mother would inform me many years afterwards – such things 'weren't intended for public consumption', nor indeed did they kiss or embrace now, but he gathered us into a general grip and a look passed between the pair of them that I knew only to be adult and fierce.

When we went indoors, the fire had set itself cheerfully ablaze, and its smoke funnelled straight up the chimney. My mother sat watching the flames and her face and hands and everything about her seemed to shine. Then she sighed and stirred herself and sent Ena with me to collect the cotton Odlum's bag with the owl's eyes from the back kitchen. We flounced it by its lugs on to a chair and a brief cloud of flour flew up. My mother cut the bag's white threads and scooped smooth cupfuls from it into her enamel basin. She added buttermilk, raisins and other ingredients as required.

'Stop that,' she ordered when we pinched a piece of dough or nipped a raisin, but I pinched again – only the dough, because the raisins gave me an itchy throat.

'Sodaish,' I said.

'Soda's what makes the cake rise,' she said, sounding happier.

'You said it was the cross that made the cake rise,' I complained. 'You told me that before.'

'You were small that time and wouldn't be able to understand the real knowledge.'

'What's the real knowledge?' Ena wondered.

'The real knowledge is that bread soda causes the cake to rise, and the cake would be no use without the soda.'

'You told a lie,' I insisted, but I was thinking about my father. Games had rules and didn't he tell us rules were meant to be kept? Maybe he and my mother wanted to win their games with each other just as badly as I did when I broke the rules during my hurling matches with my brothers. Viciously I stuck my hand into the basin to spoil the perfect cross that my mother had cut. She slapped at me with her hand but she had forgotten that it was holding the bread knife which smacked my thumb knuckle so it started to bleed.

Immediately she put my hand to her mouth and kissed it. Her face looked startled. Blood got on to her lips and she told me sorry I don't know how many times as she bathed the cut in iodine and applied a plaster to it. Then the house grew quiet and the clock on the mantelpiece filled up the space with its loud tick.

'Industry' seemed to be one of my parents' favourite words. The only sure way to win their praise was by 'showing industry' around the house and farm and workshop. Dust, which jumped out early at me from the heart of all their beloved 'industry', was my department. I swept the kitchen floor using a broom known as 'the twig', whose brightly patterned fastenings made me think of a tepee and whose long green straws sometimes broke with a pluck of dust. I used the goose-wing duster and the fire shovel to tidy the hearth and carried the bucket of ashes out beyond the cotoneaster hedge where an old scabby pine tree grew horizontally. I rag-wiped my father's boots and used another rag to knead dubbin into them. I bundled wood shavings from under the workbench into bags for bedding for the calves and sloshed with a yard brush around the leaky wooden barrel where the flitches of bacon were kept.

My jobs of sweeping and cleaning brought me up close and personal with small discoveries along the way: ants in a sand-heap, a nest of millipedes amid the potato beds, a clutch of pink and hairless baby mice under the bandsaw. Often I would skive off to look into hedges or rabbit burrows or simply into thin air. The vividness of leaf and nesting bird drew my attention. Crows conversing at morning and evening in Joe Clarke's rookery seemed to express for me the ancient thoughts of the trees themselves. I scaled the sides of water barrels and leaned, forgetting the ache in my arms, where whirligig beetles describing figures-of-eight offered their alternative take on the world.

But things weren't always what they seemed. I saw a wisp of flame rise from the ash-pit and assume the shape of a red squirrel as it licked along the trunk of the old Scots pine. In the wooden granary box I saw a rat – standing on its hind legs and baring its teeth – grow as large as a kangaroo. And I saw a fox leap out through one of the windows of the workshop without shattering the glass or making the least sound.

'Tall tales,' my mother said.

'Sometimes that lad can't tell which end of him is on the ground,' my father concurred.

Mrs Heagney, whom everybody thought wise because she knew how to fill in complicated government forms and had home cures for ailments, regularly called to our house. I liked her not just because she was my godmother but because she had a musical voice that made you calm just by listening to it. Her thin-rimmed glasses gave her face a watery look, and when I asked if she was born with them, as she was with the dislocated hip, my mother told me it was time for the joking to stop. Then there followed a merry-go-round of questions from Mrs Heagney to me – about the things I liked to do, the funniest thing I ever saw, the strangest thing . . .

'Do you ever feel sad or afraid when you see strange things?' she finally asked.

'I feel happy.'

'He'll grow out of it,' she said, turning abruptly to my mother and putting her hand on her arm as I'd seen her do when talking about raw onion being a cure for chilblains or earache, or goose grease being a help for arthritis, or flannel a preventative for a cold in the chest. 'Children can suffer from overactive imaginations, just the same as adults might suffer from big notions.'

I was given extra work to do. My first job was to open the shed door and release my mother's gaggle of geese each morning. They would waddle to the apron of the field and, as if acting on a prearranged signal of their own, take to the sky in a whirr of wings and a gabble of voices. I would watch until they'd flown – a clamorous and creaking cloud – to the furthermost reaches of the Callows. There they would graze until nightfall before ascending again and landing back among us with congratulatory cheers passing between them.

I saw the serpent in the gander's long neck and heard the serpent's voice in his warning hiss.

My mother kept a sharp eye out for goose eggs and sent me to collect them. She cleaned their shells by means of bread soda and a damp cloth. Then she numbered each, depending on when it was laid, using a pencil. Finally she buried the eggs in a bucket of oats whose coldness helped preserve them. Each time she intended to make a cake or an omelette, she would hold up an egg to the light to determine if it was still edible. 'Candling,' she called it.

She also kept hens, and through winter we ate their eggs for breakfast – but what seemed nearly more important to us was to save the shells for the spring festival which, our parents told us, had been celebrated in one form or another since God's old time. A few days before the start of May my father would chop down a small sally tree from the side of the meadow and 'plant' it on the front lawn. We would pick primroses from the ditches and Ena and Bridie would weave them among the sally's freshly leafed twigs.

'Now it's time to crown the Maypole,' my mother would say.

She would watch with her arms folded across her apron and a smile on her face while we placed the eggshells on the branchlets and yelped and whooped – the last of the primitives – and my father would emerge from the workshop to caper among us with wood shavings in his hair as we danced our Maypole dance.

Then it was work again. Ena and I were entrusted with bringing the surplus hen eggs for sale to Owenie Connolly's shop. 'Don't attempt to break one,' my mother would warn after wrapping each in newspaper and placing them all in a big, durable shopping bag patched blue and purple – but always one egg broke itself, and just as surely we were forgiven.

One day when I was about eight or nine my mother put a hen's neck under the broom-handle, stood on the handle and pulled the hen's legs until its neck was broken. I watched its final rhythmic flutterings as she held it by the legs away from her.

'I'll never again eat hen meat,' I told her, not recognising the sound of my own voice.

'The hen had to be killed,' she said. 'Else we will go hungry because there is hardly any money now.'

'But Daddy's always busy. Himself and Tommy are never finished making things – then they go into the office and count the pounds.'

'That's where you and I are heading right this minute,' she said, dragging me with one hand and carrying the dead hen in the other.

She plonked the hen on the makeshift table and turned me round towards where three thick wires with bunches of dockets and bills pressed on to each stuck out from the wall. She took a wad of papers from one wire, leafed through them and spread them in her hands before my eyes.

'Lattitats,' she said. 'Take a good look at them. Sent to hurling clubs near and far; hurling clubs from here to Cork. Dozens of hurls taken by them and none paid for. If we're lucky, some of them might pay next Christmas. Or pay only if a new batch is delivered. I guarantee you some of them won't ever pay. And the bills owing to the Forestry and the ESB – no fear but those bills will have to be paid, and on time too. As for some of the farmers around here putting their hands in their pockets to cover the cost of the wheel of a cart or even a spade-handle or a rake – they'd expect you to live on the wind.'

Her rosy cheeks grew redder as she spoke and the

redness spread over her entire face. Looking at the redness felt the same for me as a physical hurt. I thought of how my Uncle Joe had gone to America to make a better living, and of my father's big hands with cuts and bruises on them, and I felt my own face redden.

My mother fell quiet just as suddenly as she had grown loud and the redness faded to two endearing roses again. 'We won't go hungry,' she said after taking a few deep breaths. 'Even if the money's short, we'll always have the hens and their eggs, and the geese for special occasions, and the goose eggs too.'

Her mention of the geese becoming food gave me the urge to run, but she said I might as well take to my heels because the job she had to do now to prepare the hen for cooking might not be pleasant. In the end I surprised us both by staying.

First she poured hot water over the feathers to soften them. Tuft after tuft gave under her hands with an odd, ripping sound. The dimpled skin steamed, and then the giblets and entrails all but turned my stomach. The craw, packed with grains of sand and seed pickings, was sad to look at, but sadder still the series of eggs she removed from the hen's hind quarters – one egg wearing a clean brown shell, one pouched in what resembled pale paper, one a yolk, and one just beginning.

I thought over the hen's life, the way her head would dart sharp-eyed, the half-barrel where she laid her eggs and the loft where she roosted. I remembered when she had first arrived – as a little chick – together with the rest of the brood, in a cardboard box that my father had brought on the carrier of his bike from John Joe

Broderick's pub in Kilrickle, where the bus had delivered it from Dublin.

The box had air vents on its sides and big print saying 'Elm Park Hatcheries' and 'three-day-old chicks' and 'Fragile: Handle with Care'. The cardboard's odds and ends were tricked open and the chicks lifted from snug compartments lined with shavings that looked far more civilised than the shavings in the workshop.

'Rhode Island Reds,' my mother said.

We set the chicks on the kitchen floor after rubbing them against our faces and inhaling their mealy smell. We delighted in their honey-coloured fluffiness and laughed at the way they tried to pick imaginary specks off the floor.

'That's a trick they learned from the pigeons on the pavements of Dublin,' my father said.

We let their drowsy cheeps dwindle into quietness as they basked in the all-night heat of the open fire.

'The world is a tough place for all its creatures,' my mother said now, soaping and washing her hands. 'If the hen had to live wild, she wouldn't last a wet day. Wild creatures don't get much chance to grow old.'

'I don't care,' I said back. 'I will never again eat hen meat in all my born days.'

'All well and good; you can please yourself.'

Hours later the smell of cooking coaxed me in to sit where she had put my meal in its usual place alongside everyone else's, and though nobody passed any remarks about the earlier row, it hurt me to break my promise and eat.

The cuckoo flower.

'Oh, that one's supposed to be bad luck if you take it into the house,' my mother said, so we left it where it showed four pink petals and a greeny yellow heart.

The devil's bit scabious.

'No,' my mother said, examining the bluish-purple blossom, 'I don't know what it's called either.'

I learned cowslip, white clover, oat-grass, creeping buttercup, meadow barley, meadowsweet and – floating at the tranquil edges of the croaking, churning quagmire – watercress and forget-me-not. When it came to the rarest Callows flower, bell-shaped and creamy white and hidden among the prevailing browns and greens, I would have to wait, as with the devil's bit scabious, until a book identified the 'summer snowflake'.

The Callows was big when I was small. It was also entirely treeless, apart from a few diminutive blackthorn bushes nibbled by the wind as much as by any grazing animal. It had never been ploughed or treated with fertiliser, and this gave its range of highly specialised plants and animals a chance to survive. Its rivers, too small to carry names, trickled quietly along in summer but when they flooded after heavy rain all I could do was gawp at the force of the fresh current that linked them to the main river flowing across Foxhall Little and away outside the reach of my thoughts. I'm certain that the further back I go into my childhood, the slobbier, wetter, more truly itself the Callows becomes.

Several harsh-throated, drab-plumed birds depended on the Callows. Greenland geese flying in V shape made weary-sounding, high-pitched cries and the creaking of their wings – together with their feral smell – filled my head. Shyer than my mother's geese, they wheeled their large white-fronted bodies about and chose to land well away from where I stood. Whooper swans stuck out their black and yellow beaks, hissing a warning as I skirted the turlough. Golden plovers, more white than gold, reeled in flocks, resembling miniature pieces of flickering litter as their bodies caught the sunlight. Wild ducks, the males with their vivid plumage, dipped and dabbled. The corn-crake broadcast his arrival in late spring by 'serenading' the world night after night, his voice harsher than two rusty nails being scraped together.

Some birds stayed all year. The curlew rose almost straight up and made me feel melancholy by the way he called his own name as he glided back to Earth. The sound of the snipe's drumming tail feathers always stopped me in my tracks, and his zigzag flight easily de-ceived my eye. The skylark dwindled to a heavenly dot, singing as he rose.

'Closer, closer,' the quagmire croaked when my mother let me go alone. I would step and thrill and step until my wellingtons got stuck. More than once I had to scramble back or even step out of them in order to escape. I gave up this game the day one wellington slowly filled with mud and sank without trace.

Increasingly the Callows became a place of respite where I could wander about. I never felt less lonely than when alone there. Often I felt sad as a child, the sadness of disappointment. I wondered what the disappointment was. Maybe, I told myself, it involved the waiting that had to happen before I could do the 'great thing' for which

I had been born and would be remembered. Maybe it included the worry of being responsible for this great achievement, the nature of which I had not the least inkling.

Mostly I tried to coax the sadness to behave itself the way I might Jack, our jet-black pony, a kicker and a biter. Everyone must carry the disappointment that is part of them, I decided. But in the Callows the disappointing mope in my heart would shrink and I'd find exhilaration by sprinting barefoot and fast. A salt taste tanged my mouth and heat rose behind my ears; sometimes a stitch jabbed at my heart. Later, a similar abandon erupted in fights with other boys – the thrill of landing a telling blow, of ending a pent-up frustration. In my teens the drumbeat and the squawking of an electric guitar across the darkness from the dance carnival at Mullagh Cross also tapped into this sensation as powerful and primal and worth bringing on.

The Callows let me live in the moment and the moment could run and run until I completely forgot myself or, for that matter, other people's opinions of me. I was in my own manner 'forgetting human words', as W. B. Yeats said of Synge. I see now that I didn't have even the most basic sense of how to care for myself. I went without a coat in rain or frost no matter how often my mother might advise me to wear one. The cold and the wet and the pain served as balm against the sadness I felt. They couldn't stop me from exulting each time I sprinted and turned and sprinted again.

Years later, when I was a young teacher, I worked with boys who reminded me of myself as a child. They, too, went without. Some, unlike me, lived in utter poverty or wilful neglect. Others suffered a lack of physical affection similar to my own. Cold and hunger were second nature to them. They had far more genuine excuses for being difficult or disruptive than I ever had; but I still recognise the boy I was, the boy who thought himself king of the Callows and who would happily have thrown away the blanket of mist and the cold kiss of a frog for the touch of human warmth that wasn't given – not out of any meanness on the part of my parents, for they didn't have a scrap of meanness in them, but because in the way of that time such things just weren't done.

My need deepened as I entered my teens. At first I cycled to and from St Brendan's College in Loughrea. Cycling meant breezes and drenchings, but I refused to wear an overcoat. Cycling also meant avoidance of talk, especially with girls. And when the bus took the place of the bike, the driver – his big fleshy face growing incandescent – said go up the road to Castlenancy or I won't stop for you. There they were – the girls, their long hair shining and the shape of their breasts and thighs suggested behind the ruck and pucker of convent uniforms. I stole looks at them, racked my brain trying to think of something smart to say. If I could only speak the first sentence . . . but no, I looked away again, stayed dumb for five years, give or take, and the girls stayed dumb with me.

'Look down,' the wet meadow whispered.

Black oily goo oozed from a wound in one place, while in another a seepage of glorious rusty orange happened. I saw feathers scattered where a fox or hawk had struck, and a crow standing on a dead sheep's head, trying to lever out its eye. I didn't wonder about ugliness or beauty, cruelty or compassion, or if I did the Callows wasn't bothered.

Nor was it bothered when one spring a group of about twenty men arrived with nets – an extensive network of nets – and used thin rods to set them in place in the shape of a huge, open-mouthed pen. The men spread out along the perimeter of the Callows and beat the vegetation, shooing and hallooing. Hares rose and ran ahead of them until eventually there was a drove of maybe a hundred. These were flocked into the pen, where they frantically scrabbled against the netting even as it closed on them. They would be used at coursing events in various country towns where most, if not all of them, would be torn asunder by competing hounds.

I felt powerless. The big world couldn't be kept away. Its entertainments were the same as its hungers: they required to be fed. A small dread started in me there. The future would happen, changing everything, including myself. I understood at some basic level that I would have to leave when the future came. My only solution was to immerse myself ever more deeply in the Callows.

At each visit I would lift the large flat stone that lay at the Callows' edge. There I might find a slug the colour of a lemon drop, a centipede that resembled a frazzled piece of twine, or a harvestman taking slow, articulated steps as if he were a flimsy wound-up toy. They couldn't stand the light of day and maybe that's why I loved them – they were shyer even than me.

Then I would enter the cold, queasy pottage of what I would later describe in a poem as 'land aspiring to be water; water wanting to be land'. It had the raw look of a place still beginning. It didn't hold out much hope of anything remarkable. But if you leaned into it, if you stayed quiet enough for long enough, its creatures would forget you and make free. So I heard the pheasant hiccoughing as though drunk with sunset, and I found the eels – collectively if implausibly known as 'a fry' – slithering their way across the waterland.

One evening I dug below the dank mat of roots and soil and clutched up a fistful of white dripping clay. It was marl, but I didn't know that then. Slowly I crumpled its gritty sponge and found isolated on my palm three small egg-shaped shells. Smooth and whorled and beautiful to my eye but, after holding on to them for a day or two, I gave them to my mother. She could hardly have looked happier if I had given her a pearl necklace.

'Maybe the Callows was a lake,' she suggested. 'Maybe water snails lived there long ago.'

'But when was that?'

'Oh, not since Adam was a boy.'

She let the shells drop into the torn pocket of her apron where she assured me they would be safe, and I have no recollection of her ever mentioning them beyond that.

The Callows stayed with me long after I'd grown up and 'become sensible'. Its landscape turned into thought. I wanted to preserve its sights and sounds and smells the way I tried to restrain three pheasants in a furze clump once, 'flocking' them with my hands for several minutes until finally they burst upwards past my chest and face to escape. Nearly four decades later I recalled:

the marl excavations: white, with small
tell-tale shells remembering a lake
where the Callows found its first
foothold – and where your heart's pangs
are shallow waves, breaking still.

My mother had become old and enfeebled by the time
I wrote these lines, laid up in Portiuncula Hospital after
yet another stroke, one more sweeping of the ground from
under her. I had drawn the bed curtain across, sat with her
through the night. I stayed awake listening to her breath,
her scraping restlessness, and staring at the picture of a
Callows meadow scene patterned on the curtain itself.
Flowers aplenty there, patches of water, tall grasses.

Towards dawn I held her wrist while the doctor
clumsily took blood. Some blood squirted from his syringe
on to the curtain where it formed a black flower among
the lightening colours of the wetland meadow – one more
beauty to add to the forty-plus species per square metre
that river meadows are capable of supporting. I thought
of the many walks she and I had taken together. And I
found myself wishing for the shells back – or maybe for
the moment of offering them to her again.

My Uncle Tommy was fair-haired and thin-faced and
bony and brisk. He had just two names for us. We
were 'toppers' when we ran even the simplest errand
for him. Then he would give us Oatfield toffees or a
tanner or a thruppeny bit. We became 'schemers' if he
caught us tipping pebbles into the two-hundred-gallon

diesel tank or tapping out what we took to be tuneful improvisations on its broad, slightly sloped shoulders with sticks or stones or with the flats of our hands. But whether in praise or in reprimand, his voice always stayed loud.

'He shouts to hear himself,' my mother would say. 'It's the racket of the sawmill and the bandsaw which has deafened him.'

'He's deaf,' my father would assert, 'only when he hears something that doesn't suit him,' but all I could say was that our plump, far-sounding barrel music provided one of our uncle's biggest irritations.

One day a quarrel arose between the two brothers while they were in the workshop, both of them feeling the pinch over the lack of money coming in and neither of them – in our classic family tradition – wanting to be seen as ungenerous.

'We might as well work for jawbone hire,' my father said – meaning only for the food they ate – and this triggered the argument.

'I'll go,' Tommy announced, downing tools. 'There's not enough work here for the two of us.'

'You won't go anywhere.'

'Joe was right to peg off to America where decent people get well paid for hard work,' Tommy said, and then my father declared that what belonged to one of them belonged to all, the same as always.

'You have your family to feed,' Tommy asserted, softening. 'Anyway, I won't be stuck.'

He had recently inherited a farm in Newtowndaly, but my father wouldn't hear of him going and so they sorted it out simply by leaving it alone because they were friends as well as brothers.

A glance at Tommy's left wrist told us that something was odd about it. He'd been helping his brothers at the start-up of the business in the late 1930s when an accident happened. They had bought a second-hand bandsaw, at a cost of sixty pounds, from Cahill's of Gort. A lorry delivered it to the gate. Since the saw weighed over two and a half tons, they resolved to move it on rollers into the workshop. As they were shunting it, a roller skewed and the weight bore down on the crowbar Tommy was using and caused his wrist to break. The bones failed to knit properly and each time he leaned into the tricky task of cutting planks or the even more fraught process of 'ribbing' a hurley – tapering and thinning its flanks and bas so there would be less hardship for the planer – he was reminded of the calamity of his first day as a carpenter. Still the wrist never impeded his skill or his appetite for work.

With the row between them forgotten and the demand for hurleys and farm implements slow, Tommy and my father turned their attention to other tasks. The days were growing shorter, and an important winter job involved the servicing of the various tools and machines. Plough planes and bull-nosed planes, spokeshaves and breast braces, the bandsaw and bow saws all might require an overhaul. Then there were the clamps and chisels, routers and rounders, and the vintage Disston handsaws with the maple leaf of Canada on their wooden handles, though my father said the first Disston saws had been made in Philadelphia.

I was supposed to be 'a dependable note-taker' so I was given the job of listing new stock, which would be purchased in Treacy's of Killimor and would replace the worn-out or the irreparable. My brother Simon helped by whetting the smaller cutting implements on the emery wheel which I had refused to spin when I was an infant. New bandsaw blades were ordered from Hendron's of Dublin and arrangements made to send the worn-out blades for doctoring.

'The spokeshave is ideal for paring hurleys,' my father told us one day, his hurry fading as he handled the various implements. 'The plane is a rough merchant. It sweeps the board. The chisel comes in different shapes and sizes for different jobs. This one's a gouge and that one there is a slick. Some of them are refined; others you dunt with the heel of your hand. But the spokeshave has such a delicate cut you'd nearly say it respects the wood. It shaves to the thickness of a fingernail – half a millimetre – at a stroke. You could see your way around corners' – he meant the corners in a piece of wood – 'with a spokeshave.'

He explained that wood is made of fibres and that these are perforated with many tiny pores through which it breathes and sweats. In fact we could smell the sweating and breathing wood round about us. 'Ash has hardly any smell,' he continued, 'and oak is generally mild, though it can be sour as a cat's piss. Larch holds a small whiff, but the tar-and-turpentine smell of the lovely Scots pine – aah, that's the dominant one.'

Yes, the wood smell emanated from the workshop just as the smell of fresh loaves emanated from Hope's bakery in Loughrea. The hurleys, the clean lengths for handles of farming implements, the stakes and planks, all were breathing and in that sense at least seemed still alive. The sawdust and shavings, maybe even the motes of dust that floated on the air, exuded their particular perfumes.

'Now,' Tommy would say at each observation. And I found myself lingering because my father often used human terms to describe machines and gadgets that seemed the height of beauty, and because I relished the language he spoke while he was being a philosopher. His words were plain, and said what they meant, but they possessed also what I would later appreciate as a merited insight.

If I enjoyed listening to carpentry language, Simon preferred to handle the implements and discover how they worked. And my youngest brother, Vincent, would rummage about before making his own rudimentary version of what was to become a long line of adaptations or inventions to do with implement and workshop. His very first effort was a scraper of glass about four inches square and fitted with a wooden handle – a child's spokeshave.

Winter was a good time for felling ash trees. Their bareness made it easier to access them, while axe and saw cut cleaner when there was less sap. 'It takes a whole year to season one inch of thickness in hardwood trees such as oak, ash or elm, the three finest timbers in Ireland,' my father said.

He usually bought trees close to home, but he also travelled to Roscommon, Westmeath, Tipperary and Clare for ash, the only wood considered to hold the right balance of sturdiness and flexibility for the job hurleys had to do. A harvest of timber secured and seasoning in the sawmill yard meant that he could plan for the year ahead.

His winter 'timber expeditions' were famous, though he himself never spoke about them. In 1947, when the River Shannon had frozen over, he and his brothers drew logs along the ice by a system of ropes pulled by horses walking the bank. Nearer home, at Coone's house, the sight of his tractor rearing up on its back wheels as he dragged down a tree using a wire rope became the talk of all who witnessed it. On a third trip – and this deserves to be true even if it's a neighbour's invention – he and Paddy Joe Hough surmounted a frozen hill near Aughrim village with a trailer-load of timber by the tactic of letting the hot water from the tractor's radiator spill on to the road as they drove, so melting the ice.

Unfailingly, at three-month intervals throughout my childhood a batch of documents listing the woods where trees were available for felling would arrive from the forestry section of the Department of Agriculture. One morning in or about my tenth year, Tommy raised just such a document towards the drab bulb-light and tried to decipher its spidery print. My father leaned alongside him, taller and sturdier, black-haired where Tommy was fair, and between them they recited the names of various woods where 'stands' of timber were available for sale. They chose a 'lot' on offer near Kilbeggan – 'Thirty cubic metres of ash timber suitable for hurley making and commercial use,' with the standard proviso that 'some trees may contain foam rot'. Under the notice, contact details for the forester were written, and the reminder 'Treetops for firewood reserved for the Minister.'

'A pity there's nothing can be got a bit nearer home,'

Tommy said after they had debated back and forth for a while.

'Go and ask your mother to come out,' my father told me eventually.

Reddish clouds showed behind the dark shapes of the cypresses and I heard the racing sound of Seán Hanrahan's tractor as it finished rotavating the oat stubble. The gliding arc of its lights as it sped along the headland of the Old Tillage field shone between bushes.

'Are Simon and Vincent with ye in the shed?' my mother asked.

'No.'

She flew into a panic and hurried ahead of me to the workshop. My father and Tommy turned towards her and there were ructions while we searched high and low until Hanrahan's tractor came clattering its echo back off the gable wall and my two brothers dismounted, helped by Seán. Both of them grinned, flush-faced, and before my mother could complain to him, Seán drove away out the road, waving cheerfully through the cab window.

'When I'm big,' Vincent announced – he was about five at the time – 'I'll own a tractor and I'll be the king of the world.'

We all laughed, even my mother. Tommy patted Vincent's head and proclaimed us 'toppers one and all'.

'What do you think, Mary?' my father asked, showing her the lot for sale in Kilbeggan, but she barely glanced at the document and said aren't you the best judge, haven't you decided already? Then she returned to the house with my brothers in tow and my father didn't speak for a while – he had to put her words in his pipe and smoke them.

A check was made on the toll of the year's attrition on the tractor, the great leather belt and the circular saw used for the heavy cutting in the mill. Tractor oil was changed, plugs sanded, and – my favourite job – a grease gun used to pump lubricant into little warts on the tractor's body. Their name – nipples – made me smirk. My father tightened the brackets, known as 'crocodile teeth', that fastened together the two ends of the leather belt. He tested the saw's whet with his thumb and determined, as he did every year, that it required to be freshly ground down so it could bite deeper in the course of its spin.

One day during the winter of the tree-felling in Kilbeggan, he cycled to Kilrickle to make an order for a new disc saw as a back-up, from McQuillan's of Dublin. Tommy went to the workshop and set about cutting a few bits of timber for fuel, while the rest of us, feeling perished, returned to the kitchen.

Shortly afterwards a knock came to the door. Tommy stood there, death-pale, his left hand – the wrist of which he had broken years earlier – pouring blood. 'Any chance of a towel, Mary,' he said, his voice more quiet than we'd ever heard it before. 'I had a bit of an accident.'

She got a towel and he wrapped it around his injured hand. He thanked her and walked down the path, stepped into his car and drove the thirteen miles to Portiuncula Hospital. The doctors managed to save his hand, to patch and mend the sinews that had been deeply severed between thumb and forefinger.

'I turned off the power,' Tommy said, trying to make sense of it all later. 'I went to pick a chip of wood that was catching the blade . . .'

'Don't you know the blade takes its time about stopping?' my father said, but his brother raised his bandaged hand as if warding off a ghostly blow. 'I'm finished with this accursed bandsaw,' he said, his voice recovering its loudness. 'And you will finish too if you have an ounce of sense in your head. Leave it, leave it – it's a deathtrap.'

We slowly got over the shock of Tommy's accident. A living still had to be made, my father told my mother. We could hear their urgent, not always muted, voices downstairs for some nights afterwards. They were discussing the timber for sale in Kilbeggan and the fact that Tommy wouldn't be there to help.

'I worry about . . .'

'No need.'

'Will you promise . . . ?'

The sprinkling of holy water over us which my mother insisted on, to our amusement and my father's blithe unawareness, didn't seem to ease her fret. An added consideration now was that he and the men who helped him would have to find lodgings near the wood rather than returning home each evening.

'Bid for the timber,' she said.

He wrote to the forester, his script full of fancy flourishes, though he showed no delight in putting the fancy hat on the letter T as he usually would have done. And I could see by his and my mother's faces that the price they offered felt bigger than the numbers they had written down.

The sawmill plate saw waited to be ground and sharpened but – now without Tommy – my father first tackled the smaller if no less dangerous job of rounding handles for farm implements. We all came to watch the rounder in action, my mother saying that maybe by dint of our being there nothing bad would happen. The curved, adjustable blades revolved inside a casing of iron that was bolted on to a bench. The bandsaw motor powered everything. My father fed the square-edged lengths of timber in at one end and out they came rounded and smooth at the other.

'There's a satisfaction about it,' he told my mother after all was done. 'There's a kind of rightness.'

'You'll be staying at the timber so,' she said, turning from him.

We carried the plate saw to the workshop as best we could. There it was nudged into position for grinding. The back axle of a broken-down car had been converted for this purpose. A sandstone disc was affixed where one of the car-wheels would have been; a timber pulley took the place of the other. The axle was bolted into a heavy beam on top of the metal table. The sandstone disc spun at a rate of two thousand revs per minute. Water trickling from a tank suspended above the interface between saw and spinning sandstone kept, as my father put it, the steel from 'losing its temper'.

He leaned in with keen eye and careful movement, his gloved hands managing the saw so the notch between its first two teeth came in contact with the sandstone. Showers of sparks sprayed whitely under and about the sunken space. The dimly lit workshop, with a single dust-coated bulb strung on a flex above the water tank, accentuated the splendour of the streaming sparks. It was a short-lived glory, for no sooner would the starry sparks blitz forth than they lapsed back, to be replaced by fresh, equally short-lived constellations.

The sounds played on us, constant grinds and groans as tiny filaments of metal were sheared and sloughed off. Yet behind the rasps and hardships melodious notes rose and fell, surprising our ears, attuning us, so we listened out for more. Pings, clinks, jingles, tinkles, rattles, bongs and gongs filled the air as the long evening passed deep into night through a series of bell reverberations.

Afterwards, an assortment of hatchets was whetted. A strange smell permeated the workshop, the hellish smell of burnt steel and spent sandstone which would linger for days before the aroma of wood wafted back into place.

We returned the saw to the mill and elevated it on to the driveshaft. My father placed a file in front of its teeth and spun the saw by hand.

'Two high teeth,' he said.

These he filed back flush with the others. A tall implement known as a G cramp was used for setting the saw's forty-two teeth.

'You bend one tooth to the left and the next to the right,' he told us, illustrating what he meant. 'The gap you create lets the saw have enough space to cut the timber without becoming choked or overheated.'

The word he gave for the width of the cut made by the saw was 'kerf'. The circular saw had a kerf of about one-quarter of an inch. 'At least one-tenth of each log will be turned to sawdust by the kerf,' he said.

Not that the sawdust would go to waste. We shovelled it into plastic fertiliser sacks and, just before the start of the New Year, a restaurant-owner from Galway paid one pound per bag for it because, as he remarked, 'it's ideal for smoking fish'.

'Will you go to Owenie's and get me a few messages?' my mother asked. 'You can buy sweets for yourself if you want.'

This was the most familiar road of my childhood – to and from school, to and from herding the cattle in Mullagh Beg, to and from hurling practice in the big field beyond Mullagh Cross. But now night was falling as I headed out, a reluctant eleven-year-old, to buy the 'red packet' tea – Rajabaree – my mother had requested, and the ten Gold Flake cigarettes that would last my father for a week and a half.

Things sounded louder in the dark. The breeze sighed and relented. A sudden little thrash – a bird or a mouse or a rat – stilled me for a moment, then again my footsteps echoed on tarmacadam and I heard the steady whisper of my pulse behind my ears.

Bushes and briars clung to either ditch. Primroses, golden-hearted in their radiance, seemed to shine ever more intensely as the darkness thickened. I often had a sense of something strange about to happen, and on my night-walks this feeling invariably accompanied me. I could put names to all the farmhouse lights, steady and scattered in the blacked-out distance. The smells of the teacher's pansies and tulips wafted up over her wall and her big, rust-coloured sheepdog barked. A recently installed porch-lamp bloomed whitely across the fields as I reached the height beyond the hairpin bend. There stood the Master's residence, its prize apples ripening behind a high thicket.

I came to the church and caught the faint gleam of its stained-glass windows and the pale outline of the Celtic cross that dominated the smaller monuments in the priests' graveyard. A bat zinged past my ear, unnerving me slightly. An old woman whom I didn't recognise emerged through the heavy pine door, gathered her bicycle where it leaned against the church wall, stepped daintily on to a pedal and eased away downhill without saying a word.

My mother had given me a five-naggin bottle for refilling with holy water but I didn't want to be caught dead carrying it into Owenie's. I plonked it behind the font in the church porch and headed out again.

Everything held a memory. There was the ridge of tar against which I bumped my big toe in barefoot weather, and twisting above it the elderberry bush whose bitter juice purpled my lips in autumn. Beyond a rusty gate the meadow where I'd dived to catch a grasshopper and come up with a pocket watch stretched away towards the furze bushes under whose thorns I burned my mouth while smoking a crooked pipe. Across the road from the church the beech trees seemed to whisper about the windfall burrs and cupules I'd sifted through for nuts that might still be edible. Nearby, on a concrete pedestal with steps leading up to it, the pump that slaked my thirst on warm evenings after school continued to pretend it was a dinosaur, its spout the small head and its handle the long tail not quite touching the ground.

Just as I passed the hollow where a girl lifted her dress and said she would show me hers if I would show her mine, the cables above me started their thin piping. Owenie's grocery shop with the petrol pump and the blue and yellow Maxol sign held high on a dinged pole and the wide clean gable window came into view. I nodded at the bags of flour and the trays of chocolates and the Fizz Bombs and the Black Maria liquorices and the shelves of boxes and the bacon slicer and the array of foodstuffs in tins and the smell of fresh bread, and Owenie massaged his broad brow and said God but you're out late, what can I get you?

He handed me the tea and the packet of Gold Flake and then took a big, square-faced bull's-eye jar and twisted off its lid. He fluffed a brown paper bag open with his fingers and placed it on the Avery weighing scale with the numerous demarcations and the super-sensitive needle. His elbow jerked as he dug the scoop into the jar and chucked the bull's-eyes into the bag. He studied the needle, nudged a few extra bull's-eyes in, and spun the bag closed using both hands. 'That's it now,' he said.

I picked the bag up by one dog-ear, paid him and left.

The night felt colder suddenly and I remembered when Ena and Simon saw a white mist rising with a whoosh above the bushes and came home pale and frightened. I broke into a gallop and told myself it was just for the heck of it. Past the Maxol sign I ran, past the level field where the showbands played in the six-pole marquee, past the water pump, past the church before I realised my mistake and turned reluctantly back.

The door was hard to push open. I fumbled for my mother's bottle and delved it into the holy water font where it filled with a bubbling noise. I looked through the porch glass, towards the long central aisle, the small red sanctuary lamp flickering as though about to drown, the greyish marble altar encircled by the communicants' rail. A strange feeling gripped me and I peered in more closely, all but pressing my nose to the glass. A black shape appeared to be standing on the altar. I gaped, my whole body tingling now. Could it be Georgie the beggar up to his mischief, for he was well known to sleep some nights in the organ loft? But Georgie was stooped and shrunk where this figure stood tall and imposing. Suddenly the figure raised its arms – seeming to open as it did so a crinkled and convoluted fan of webbing – and lifted off the altar and glided headlong towards me down the empty, dim-lit nave. I scampered from the porch, leaving the bottle dunked in the font, and fled homeward, scarcely noticing that the night had begun to spit rain.

'Don't you know well it's your imagination,' my mother said, handing me a sympathetic drink of hot chocolate after I tumbled out the story to her. 'The church is a sacred place and nothing bad would ever happen to a person there.'

'I saw it.'

'You imagined it.'

There was no talking to her. But now when I look back along the most familiar road, I wonder if I imagined not just the incident in the church but everything down to the gallery of our faces, the little world that was matter-of-fact in each farmhouse out on its own with the door unlocked and no need to knock when you happened to call. I look back and see how my whole life amounts to a dream. But, for all that, I still mourn the loss of the beautiful, fiercely 'real' hallucinations that entranced me in early childhood.

'You just imagined it all,' my mother said, reasonable as could be, but in that kitchen on that particular night and for several nights afterwards I feared the dark figure and prayed with desperate fervour to be spared his re-appearance.

Mrs Heagney visited on my twelfth birthday and handed me a slim, velvety box. Inside there was a fountain pen, navy blue with a golden nib and a golden lever.

'It's too good to use,' I told her.

'You'll get used to it,' she said with a brusque tinkle in her voice and I caught the soft, earnest look behind the shimmer of her glasses as she showed me how to unscrew the pen at the middle to reveal the ink gut. This set me thinking of the long black insect that lived under a stone in the Callows, and I told her as much.

'Oh, indeed,' she replied. 'I didn't forget to bring the jar of ink.'

We twiddled the pieces back together and worked the lever so the pen filled with a croaking sound. I found a scrap of paper and put down the insect's name – *devil's coach-horse* – and it felt as if I had tapped into some-thing that called a halt, offered a stay, something that was meant for me.

You have to keep yourself occupied in order to be happy. So my mother said. You did this not by forgetting your-self, a knack I might hope to become good at, but by the much tougher business of forgetting *about* yourself. Her best way of doing so – she did 'indulge' occasionally in a sip of Irish Cream or a piece of Gateau cake and would chat convivially with friend or neighbour on whatever subject interested them – was to keep busy. She immersed herself in house- and farmwork and never complained if she saw it as any sort of sacrifice.

I didn't follow her advice. In retrospect, I seem to have spent much of my childhood stuck 'betwixt and between', busy staring things into a dream. I waited – in the Callows or stretched on my back on the flat porch-roof or inside the tree-trunk that lay along the path to the sawmill. Sometimes the world switched itself off while I waited. Sometimes my head might have fallen off and I would scarcely have noticed.

Yes, for a few years the tree-trunk was one of my places, though I'm at a loss still to figure what exactly I was waiting for. It was huge and hollow right through and must have lain there for a long time because it had shed its entire covering of bark and looked a sorry shade of grey. While my father and the men who worked with him stepped around it, my siblings and I used it as a tunnel, often as not. Our hands and knees scuffed its soft flesh each time we crawled through, so the tunnel grew wider with each passing year.

Eventually Ena stopped bothering with it, believing there was more dignity in simply walking past. Simon soon followed her example. Then Bridie and Vincent ignored it. By now it had grown so wide you could sit inside without having to stoop your head. I took up casual residence there, savouring the wood's spicy smell, and I found one use at least in hiding from the jobs my parents thought up when they saw me hanging about.

A heap of logs with a long-handled hatchet sunk into a chopping block occupied the area to the right of the tree-trunk. Beyond and to the left, the sawmill stood – behind the workshop but sharing a wall with it. The heavier work of cutting raw lumber was done in the mill. Loose galvanised sheets clung to its high rickety roof. You might expect the next big wind to lift and sweep them away. Big winds rose and subsided but the roof stayed put, held fast by rusty rivets driven into the rafters.

The sawmill bench consisted of two massive parallel beams of pine resting on a series of low concrete pillars. Between the beams and supported by them several wooden rollers ran. On top of the rollers the great bench or 'carriage' rested. It could be moved forwards or back-wards by turning a handle. It really acted as two benches in one, with a gap between to accommodate the circular buzz saw attached to a driveshaft at the centre of the mill and linked by means of a leather belt to the pulley of the tractor.

The sawmill was the one thing that distinguished us from neighbouring children. I remember thinking that. We could say we ran a heavy industry, a heavy rural industry quite separate from farming, and though I avoided much of the labour involved, I felt proud of the fact of the sawmill. When I wasn't in one or other of my 'dream lands', I would run wild in bouts of play with my brothers and sisters, especially during the summer. Our parents let us go, sometimes until near midnight when darkness definitely had fallen, in games of hide-and-seek that encompassed the entire farm. Because it was out of bounds as a playground, the sawmill in particular attracted us.

We loved to climb the tree-trunks that lay in clumsy heaps around the mill-yard. We scarcely recognised them as trees since they had been stripped of their crowns and branches after they were felled. Some were of pine, long and scabby and giving off a turpentine smell. Others were ash butts, stocky and smooth with moss or veins of ivy clinging to their bark. On several, the bark looked as if it had been wrapped taut over long tube-shaped bones. The various heaps offered steep gradients and sharp angles where they had slipped from the tip-up trailer. We would use them to test our balance – or indeed our nerve – until a log rolled away under us or a clattering avalanche gave no option but to jump.

Sawdust covered the ground. So much sawdust it heaped itself into dunes. My sisters used jam jars and old saucepans to make castles. Or they dug down where the sawdust became black earth and gouged out swimming pools for their dolls, or imagined them at the beach in Salthill where Uncle Mattie had once taken us on a day trip.

Simon, Vincent and I wrestled leftovers of old machines from clumps of dead nettles or from the drifting sawdust where they lay half-buried, and wielded them as weapons in pretend hand-to-hand combat.

'They're like skeletons,' Simon said.

But what odd-looking skeletons – wheel rims, mud-guards, hubcaps, exhaust pipes, engine grilles, gear-sticks, axles, scrunched-up oil drums, even skewered mirror frames whose glass had fallen out or been broken, and cast-iron seats still bolted on to pedestals that had lost their springiness. It was as if a giant had pulled so many tractors and other machines asunder and thrown the pieces heedlessly about the sawmill yard.

'The mule won't kick any more,' my father said one cold winter morning after the old Ferguson TVO tractor gave up the ghost while he was attempting to start it. 'I'm afraid we'll have to buy a newer, more powerful model.'

'A model you can afford,' my mother said.

He went to Curley's in Kiltormer to buy a 'brand new' second-hand tractor, and wouldn't be back before evening. We could do as we pleased. Except that my brothers didn't want to play. They decided instead to study the mule, whose head was cracked and whose cumbersome belly dripped thick, burnt-black oil where it slouched on its four bald tyres. The mule would spit and splutter no matter the weather, and was feared for its bad temper. Its crank-handle had broken one man's leg, caused another to lose his front teeth, and frequently sent my father flying by back-firing while he was 'giving it a swing'.

'It's finished,' Vincent said when we went over. 'We've no crane to lift it, so it'll have to be buried.'

'The same as a dead animal,' I said.

'Bury it where?' Simon wanted to know.

'Bury it here,' Vincent said. 'It won't start and the back wheels have seized up, so how can it be moved?'

'It can't be buried here,' I said. 'Here is where the steam engine is buried.'

'That yoke is bound to be rotted away if it was ever there in the first place,' Simon said.

'I bet you it's still here,' I said. 'Who's to say some day it won't get dug up?'

We eventually drifted to the front of the house to wait for my father. The three of us climbed the biggest cypress next to the boreen and used it as a lookout. Its heavy waxen leaves brushed against our faces and we got the fragrance of its rough, blue-green berries. About one-third of the way up, the trunk forked to make two thick, rounded limbs. I decided on one, followed by Vincent, while Simon chose the other. The higher we climbed, the more the branches shook. Then we could see the main road's long fall – facing us from the direction of Mullagh church – foreshortened, empty of traffic.

We waited. At last a noise began somewhere beyond the cold-looking stand of beech trees that stood to the west of the church. The noise rose to a barrel rumble. A light flickered once or twice as the church wall threw back the solid rapping of an engine. The light stretched itself to form a dazzling twin-beam of headlamps. And then we could tell him by his longish hair and his heavy overcoat, and by the odd angles his arms and elbows made as he clutched the steering wheel.

We waved and cheered but he neither saw nor heard us. The tree shook violently and I got a brief but startling topsy-turvy view of the deep-dark-blue sky with stars beginning to break through before my body did an auto adjust. Smoke gunned from the tall exhaust pipe, twisted and fell away in a vague grey-white curl. Flame-bright sparks flew as my father thundered down the long fall.

'He must be doing forty!' I shouted.

'I'd say the most he could do is twenty miles an hour,' Simon said evenly.

'What colour?' Vincent asked, too low down to see for himself.

'Grey,' I said. 'Grey with big patches of rust streaked through it.'

'Grey?'

Simon laughed and Vincent pinched the calf of my leg hard – and I had to tell him blue with orange-rimmed wheels.

My father drove in, a frown crossing his face as he pointed and beckoned before stopping and dismounting. We scrambled from our perches and hurried past the gate. His hands and lips appeared cold. He stomped warmth into his feet and swung his arms in wide flaps across his ribs. Then he smiled a charming, crooked smile.

'Well wear,' my mother, Ena and Bridie said as they came out the path.

'A humdinger,' Simon said.

And Vincent, who was already studying the quietly ticking engine, told us it was going like a clock. The mudguards trembled and at the back of each a light the same deep red as our Sacred Heart lamp glowed. The crest affixed to the tractor's forehead showed an ear of barley and a cog wheel. I watched its alluring beams extend along the boreen halfway as far as Heagney's and Hough's houses. Our shadows shifted and lurched hugely as we crossed over and back, looking at everything. Then we put our hands against the grille and the rippled glass of the cone-shaped lamps – not so much for warmth as out of a wish to be close to the engine's oddly hypnotic, jigging concert.

I was 'cured' of tractors late one evening some years later in that between time when I was no longer a child but not quite a man, while driving a load of timber home from Woodlawn. An old woman leaning on a walking stick had started crossing the road a few hundred yards ahead of us and, though we were trundling downhill at a fair speed, I didn't take much notice at first. But as we drew nearer I saw that she had stopped, still less than halfway across. I put my foot to the brake but met no resistance. I slammed uselessly, then – having no other option – veered right, to the slightly more open side, and squeezed through the narrow space between the woman and the ditch. 'Use the governor!' my father shouted from the swaying trailer at my back. The engine cut out and everybody was safe.

I haven't driven a tractor since but my head remains full of tractors. There's the blue Ford which a farmer in Kilconieron called 'the silver bullet' and used for taking his wife on romantic jaunts. There's the low, grey Styr parked on a hill which the owner would start by letting it free-wheel and then putting it in gear, so saving on battery costs. And there's the Massey Ferguson hired out for farmwork by a neighbour, Lex Bugler – prone, he would say with an endearing smile, to thirst, same as the rest of us.

Then there are the tractors my father used, ranging from the Fordson EN27 he purchased for three hundred pounds in the 1940s and used for pulling down trees, to the Fordson Super Diesel of the mid-1970s whose clock told us it had spent four thousand hours working underground at Tynagh Mine before it came to our sawmill.

But the first tractor I really took to was that spick and span second-hand blue and orange Fordson Major bought from Curley's garage after the demise of the mule when I was about twelve years old. I remember us racing out – followed by the 'big child' who was my father – to step around it in the cold clear light of the morning after its arrival. Fore and aft we stepped, momentarily half-shy of it, circling and pointing as if contending with a force field. Then we climbed and dragged ourselves aboard, and fought over the pan-shaped seat, and finally agreed to share it.

'It's not a toy,' my father said, watching on while we fiddled with switches, levers, gears and pedals. And when we turned the ignition key, the engine didn't need to be asked twice. Mumbo-jumbo it said, mumbo-jumbo, mumbo-jumbo, trembling under the power of its own arcane internal workings.

Later Mattie, the 'head beetler' of my father's family, arrived wearing his customary tweed jacket. There was an increased stoop to his tallness, and his sallow face seemed to me more deeply lined about the lips. 'It's a rickety, clickety vehicle,' he remarked, after staring open-mouthed for a long minute. 'It has enough metal in it to build a fleet of cars.'

Other callers came, farmers mostly, tired of donkey-work, worn out by the horse-drawn plough, hankering after a tractor of their own.

'What make is she?' one man asked, wrapping an arm

about the hood just as he might around the neck of his Irish dray.

'She's mighty, on'y mighty,' a second confided, sneaking a touch off the machine for luck before withdrawing his hand.

'What horsepower is she now?' a third man asked, taking all in his eye.

'Forty horsepower,' my father told him.

'I suppose she can do the work of eighty men so.'

One horsepower was said to match the strength of four men . . . but my father let it pass.

'She don't go on strike or get tired in her bones,' the man said, slapping his cap on the bonnet as though laying down a winning card at Muldoon's pub.

My father never referred to any of his tractors as 'she'. He loved them in a pragmatic rather than a fanciful way, much as he loved all manner of implements and machines. Maybe the harsh graft of timberwork, the constant possibility of breakage and let-down, helped him keep the lid on his tractor love. And after everybody had gone, the engine experts, the customers for hurleys and the borrowers of augers and chisels, he set about rendering the old mule into scrap.

First he jacked up the wheels one at a time, starting at the front. We helped him stack concrete blocks that would bear the weight as each wheel was taken off. The mule looked precarious, denuded, even faintly ridiculous. Its front-wheel ball-races and rear-wheel half-shafts were removed. Next he addressed the engine cover, the head-gasket, the engine block and the pistons. He lay on his back under the tractor where the sump – resembling a shallow basin – had to be unbolted. He 'split' the tractor by opening a circle of bolts, and forced the two sections apart. Through this gap of approximately six inches he edged out the flywheel, then the clutch, its springs and disc, until only the carcass remained.

Every part that might come in useful was placed in safe keeping.

Finally he raised a sledgehammer and swung. The first blow cracked the cast-iron belly, now puddled with oil. The second caused a shard of metal to fly. The third broke off a chunk the size of a teacup. When I looked again, blood and oil were mingling about a cut in his hand. He examined the wound for a moment and then went to the house where my mother doctored and bandaged it. He swung once more, thumping and pulverising until the mule lay in a mess of gleaming metal at our feet.

'It had to be done,' he said, and we nodded.

I thought of the steam engine lying below the oil-muddied hollows, the first of a long line of obsolescent machines, buried and unburied, for which our sawmill served as a graveyard. I had read somewhere how steam engines in the nineteenth century had inspired the development of the first tractors, and now this idea of mechanical evolution cheered me, for I could picture the steam engine hidden away yet somehow present still, a prompter and an augmenter of everything.

The scrap-dealer – wild-haired and yellow-booted and wearing corduroy trousers that were too short for him – arrived, and we loaded his van. After he had gone, my father found long-handled locking pliers lying beside the wall. They shone, being made of alloy steel, but to me their curved and serrated grinning jaws were a reminder of the wicked-looking pike I had glimpsed skulking in the shadowy waters under Clonlathan Bridge. We expected the scrap man to return and claim his tool but he never did. And then, to placate us, my father started the Fordson Major again and gave it a good rev before driving it into the shed for the night.

'Go over,' he said to me finally, 'and ask Paddy Hough if he would lend us a hand at the sawmill tomorrow.'

'Why can't you ask Simon or Vincent to go over?'

'Am I not asking you?'

Paddy Joe, a powerfully built man in his early thirties, lived two doors away. I dreaded going near his house because he delighted in frightening us. Each time we told our parents, they said 'pass no remarks on Paddy Joe, he's only making fun'.

'Welcome, young lad,' his mother said, the many lines on her face seeming to make it all the more beautiful, and I began to relax, glad that Paddy Joe didn't seem to be around.

'Was that a tractor I heard beyant at your house just now?' Mrs Hough asked.

'We are after buying a new Fordson Major.'

'It has a great pair of lungs, God bless it.'

She lit a cigarette and sat down, but I remained standing.

'Has he got rid of the other thingamajig?' she asked.

'He smashed it up. It conked out on him. The cold cracked its engine or something.'

'Ah, the cold would crack anyone's engine,' she said,

her voice lightening owing to the effect of a fresh drag on the cigarette. 'Do you want himsel'?'

'Could you ask him can he come sawing with my father for tomorrow?'

'Couldn't you ask him yoursel'?'

The voice was Paddy Joe's. He must have been listening behind the door to his bedroom and now he emerged. He was dressed in loose black trousers with a white vest tucked under his black leather belt – getting ready to go dancing. His biceps might have been sculpted by Michelangelo but his handsome face wore the devil's grin. I could tell by the way he caressed his smooth, round blue-black chin that he had just shaved. His dark eyes lit on mine and his eyebrows seemed to pop and twitch.

'Did anyone see ya comin' in?' he asked.

'No.'

'Well, be Jaysus they won't see ya goin' out neither.'

He reached for the wooden shelf above the fireplace and felt about until his fingers closed on a large knife which he drew down. It had a thick black handle and a long, slightly curved steel blade. His pig-killing knife, which I'd seen him use in plenty of farms around the parish, including our own – and his standard cry of 'lovely hurling' as the animal's screams died away came fresh to my mind. There was dust on the blade. He blew lightly and I could feel the dust tickle my neck.

'Ah, Paddy Joe, can't you lave the child alone?' his mother said.

Ignoring her, he reached again. This time his hand came down with a whetstone. I recognised, without looking, its cuboid shape worn hollow at the middle. His eyes held mine. I calculated the distance to the door but knew I wouldn't make it. He spat thinly on the whetstone and started sharpening the knife.

Snip – snup – snip – snup.

Back and forth the blade moved. His honing hand moved this way and that, his eyes still fixed on mine. Keep cool, a voice in my head said. It's not as if he's going to kill you, is it? An unusual word occurred to me, haemoglobin. It had to do with the way oxygen was transported around the body and I felt my heart hammering and my breath quickening as the blood carried the oxygen around and I said the word to myself over and over in broken syllables.

Hae-mo-glo-bin. Hae-mo-glo-bin. Hae-mo-glo-bin.

Paddy Joe had stopped sharpening. He took one sudden step and clutched me by the throat. He held me there and the knife touched my Adam's apple – a cold, flat touch.

'Tell me, ma'am,' he said to his mother, 'do ya want to save the blood or do ya mind if the floor gets a bit splashed?'

'Ah now, it's gone past a joke,' she said.

His foot crooked a white basin from under the table and jigged it over to where we both stood. 'I'll save it so,' he said. 'Waste not, want not, ha?'

My eyes rolled but my heart burned. I twisted my head up towards Paddy Joe's smooth, pitiless face and stared deep into his eyes and didn't blink. At that he twirled me away from him. 'You're too underfed. I'll give ya a year, mebbe six month.'

I shook myself and kept staring.

'Come 'ere, child of grace,' Mrs Hough was saying now. Then she proceeded to scold Paddy Joe as 'a misfortunate article' but his eyes glimmered merrily as he casually placed the knife back on its shelf. 'Tell your father I'll be over in the morning,' he said, turning and leaving the kitchen.

'Would you like a cut of bread?' Mrs Hough asked, putting her arm around my shoulder. 'A nice cut of white soda bread and strawberry jam.'

I shook my head. Mrs Hough was famous for her white soda bread and jam, but still. And then, as I half-suspected she would, she took my head-shake to mean yes.

I ate the treat, and immediately regretted eating it, and slouched away from Hough's house with my hands sunk to the elbows in my pockets. When I was about halfway home, I stopped in the middle of the boreen and after checking about me covered my eyes and concentrated very hard. Nothing doing for a while but finally I could see it – the steam engine that was buried under the ground. It seemed asleep as any fossil the Callows ever held. I concentrated until a pain pinballed around in my head and – with a grind and a groan – the metal monster thrummed and shook, spewing gouts of steam and bits of earth as it resurrected itself. Then there it was before my eyes, large as life and twice as ugly, and I saw myself driving it, leaning into the gear-shift as it clanked sluggishly forward, its broad wheels smashing weeds and pebbles and all that stood in our path, and though something in the both of us felt broken my senses sang.

That night I listened to the rain shellacking on the roof and finally fell asleep, and then the world froze solid. By morning, dense clusters of ferns and horsetails and frost flowers seemed to have become trapped inside the bedroom windowpane. I put my thumb against it and burned a clear spot through to the huddle of hay-pikes in the haggard and to the whitened fields beyond. A jagged set of icicles, each curving to a length of two or three feet, hung from the workshop roof. Downstairs in the back kitchen the water bucket offered a wafer of ice. 'That never happened before in all my memory,' my mother told us.

After breakfast we stood in the yard and wondered at the icicle tusks. With an effort Simon broke one off and I another. We started a swordfight and our breaths were visible and our voices carried far. My father laughed and Vincent, seeing his chance, drove the tractor out of the shed. Forward and back he manoeuvred until he had squared it with the sawmill.

We stooped to the unglamorous job of unrolling the leather belt. My father twisted it once across itself so that it would run with greater stability, and pressed it over the tractor pulley. Vincent reversed, putting as much stress as he dared on the belt, applying foot and hand brakes as necessary, and took the tractor out of gear. Clutch again, and a clockwise yank of a lever set the pulley spinning. The belt slid into motion, a grey, elongated figure-of-eight flowing sideways.

I moved to the middle of the mill. Above the noise of the engine I heard the whirr of the saw. Its teeth were a blur as it whipped up sawdust from the recess underneath. Simon saw a crowbar lying on the ground and tried to pick it up but the frost had sealed it fast. He and I put our four hands to it but it stayed gummed.

'Get a crowbar to shift a crowbar,' he said, taking a stake from the workshop and digging its spiked end in, levering the crowbar loose.

'Archimedes said you could feck the world out of its axis if you had a crowbar that was long enough,' I told him.

'Ah, we've job enough now to move them tree-trunks nearer the bench.'

Each trunk was about four and a half feet long. Some had stones and clay wedged between their roots. Others were slim and smooth-skinned. In all of them the ample curve of the root ensured that the hurleys would follow an unbroken grain from handle to *bas* and would therefore most likely be of top quality. We freed a tree-trunk from the weight of its neighbours and tried to roll it along the frost-starched sawdust. The trunk budged and then, more simply and soundlessly than a twig, the crowbar snapped in Simon's grip. It severed at its mid-point.

'You'll be a legend,' I told him. 'I can see the headline: "Young schoolboy shatters crowbar with bare hands".'

Unimpressed, he left the two pieces lying against the pile of tree-trunks and instead we used the tomahawk, which had a loose, hinged claw attached to its handle, to lever and turn the trunk. Together we lifted before pinching the trunk into position on the bench by means of a nail bar.

'Ah Jaysus, ye'd want to put a stir under ye,' Paddy Joe Hough shouted, giving me a jump. He spat on his hands and rolled his shoulders as he scrunched towards us in past the sawmill gate and along the slippery gravel path. 'We have a fair scatter of trees to round up.'

Not bothering to look for crowbar or tomahawk, he tilted a tree-trunk on end and waltzed it in towards the bench, following immediately with another. He'd earned the name 'Strong' from the local men, and done so by meeting every challenge head on:

'You won't lift that, Paddy Joe. No man in Ireland would be able to lift that.'

'Ah what are ya saying? Why wouldn't I lift it?'

'Start the saw!' he shouted now towards Vincent, who was determined to hold on to the job of controlling the tractor. Shortly after, my father came out and complimented us on not being idle.

'A pity you broke that, Paddy,' he said after a while, noticing the two halves of the crowbar.

'Ha?'

'A pity you broke the crowbar.'

'Jaysus, I did not break it. That's the first I saw of it – ask the young lads and they'll tell ya.'

'It was sound as a bell the last we saw of it,' I said, looking at my brothers.

'Be the cross a' Christ,' Paddy Joe swore, stepping quickly away and back again. 'Amn't I after tellin' ya I know damn all about it.'

'Bring a bucket of water,' my father said, glancing suspiciously at me. 'And bring the old saucepan while you're at it.'

The saucepan – dinged and burnt and minus its handle – was lying in the sawdust. The water came from a barrel. I dislodged a discus of ice to get it, pounding with the heel of my fist until it gave, singing to myself as I did so and still singing as I launched the discus in Al Oerter Tokyo

Olympics fashion at the snowy shoulders of the cypresses.

Skirrrr. Skaaaaaaaaaaaaarrrrrmm. Skluppp.

The huge galvanised sound of steel cleaving through wood called me back. No dictionary held words capable of catching or containing that horrendous noise. My father and Paddy Joe stuffed their ears with plugs of cotton wool against it – they hadn't yet come to the use of earmuffs – as they eased in the giant tree-butt. The top of the blade was barely visible above the timber. It reminded me of a shark's fin cutting through water. Except that a shark would never struggle the way our saw was struggling now. Smoke belched from the blade and then a spray of sparks. The belt swayed and wobbled but it didn't fly off. The tractor stuttered, recovered its powerful prattle, stuttered and prattled.

My father jerked his head in my direction. I dipped the saucepan in the bucket and splashed at the blade. Steam hissed. A mess of smoke and sparks issued up. Splash again, my father's head-nod said. Sawdust poured into the gathering place below, showing that yes, the blade was winning. The instant the tree-trunk had been split the saw gathered speed, the tractor engine raced, and the belt flowed smoothly again. The mill sounded celebratory now.

The half-trunks were halved again. The cacophony rose as before, the saw belched smoke and sparks, the water splashed, and the tractor cheered when the hardship ended. Each quarter-trunk was cut into planks from which the hurleys would be ribbed. Simon and I carried the planks two at a time to the workshop. They looked pink and disconsolate, shedding strips of bark where our fingers gripped. Each plank would be left to season on the makeshift scaffold under the rafters where they would lose their sap.

Sap was the blood of a tree. I felt sorry for all the trees that must fall so hurlers could hurl and crowds could cheer, so tables and cupboards and chairs and floorboards and ceilings and window frames and even pencils – the thousand appliances of wood – could happen. But then the haranguing noise began again and I felt sorry for my father, stooped over the blade, taking a risk at every turn.

After a while my mother came out and waved to him, but he didn't see her at first. There she was in her moss-coloured coat waving – and he in his brown study looked as serious as a professor, unaware of her. The dinner's ready, her lips said, her breath billowing into fogginess; tell him the dinner's ready.

Hearing at last, he moved towards her and made to slip his hand around her middle but, as if realising his hand's griminess, held off, and I watched the dance between them, he leaning towards her and she putting her mouth to his ear and hand-cupping the idea of the dinner into it for good measure.

Nightfall, which was really only late afternoon, brought an end to the work. The following morning we would resume, and for how many days after, each with its consumptive demands, its quirks and alarms, its blotches and hotchpotches greasing the hand and inking themselves into the mind's eye?

The Master had allowed a dispensation from school in response to a note – *For the next few days the boys will be cutting timber* – sent by my mother, but I didn't want it.

Simon, however, jumped at the prospect, as did Vincent.

With an anti-clockwise twist of a lever the belt slowed and the saw became toothily distinct again. We listened to its tetchy, clinking noises as it cooled, and then we shuffled from foot to foot and pulled our coats tighter about our throats, setting our faces against another night of hard frost.

The silence seemed touchable. I had to check myself against keeling over. I felt as if I was plummeting into an abyss.

Oooooooooooooooo . . .

A bell tolled in my ears and I knew that it couldn't be outrun. Paddy Joe tossed the last few shovelfuls of sawdust in casual movements of his shoulders and wrists, his feet making nimble bounding movements as he spread about him a saffron carpet. It hit me then. I would never be able to dance the way he could dance.

'God spare you the health,' my father said, handing Paddy Joe the day's wages.

'And yoursel',' Paddy Joe replied, stuffing the notes into his breast pocket without counting them.

The water sparkled as if alive when my father poured it into the barrel, but he didn't wait to look at it in that light. He just set off again for Keaveney's well with a bucket in either hand. I emptied my nearly three-quarter-full bucket into the barrel, stirring afresh the dark effervescence, but this time I didn't follow him. Carrying water was a bother and a bore. I kicked off my shoes because the socks had become splashed and I lay on the grass.

When the first barrel was full, he started on the second. Aside from Keaveney's well, we relied on the run-off from the roof, but there was often a shortage in summer. The lake of Loughrea wouldn't be deep enough to keep us washed and fed, my mother said. In potato-spraying season, the need for a more dependable supply grew greater than ever.

Tommie Donoghue always arrived at a fast trot with his horse and sprayer to apply the 'bluestone' wash of copper sulphate and sodium carbonate known to counter blight. He lived his working life in a state of agitated hurry, and it communicated itself to everyone around him. 'The trick is to spray in fine weather,' he would tell you in his loud, clear voice. 'But, this being the west of Ireland, you have to gauge the dry spell that might be given to you between showers.'

The sprayer was made of wood, a barrel turned on its side and mounted on the horse-cart and able to hold seventy or eighty gallons. The sprayer pump worked in response to the movement of the cart axle. When Tommie's horse took a forward step, the sprayer's pipes – which could open on to a copper arm with jets angled to spray the undersides as well as the tops of the potato leaves – would fizz as if ready to explode. The whole contraption seemed a living extension of its pressurised owner, or at the very least gave a fair impression of his frazzled temperament.

Tommie would certainly tell you he was expected else-where. His mind constantly danced forward to the task at hand on the next farm and the one after, for he had the potatoes of the entire parish to spray. Big and little we would help, ferrying bucket after bucket from the barrels to where my father lifted them splashing and dripping and Tommie poured – in great musical commotion – down the funnel of his sprayer.

'That'll do!' he'd shout, then drop the ball of bluestone in and stir with a stick before lifting the reins and clicking his tongue. The horse would strain forward and the sprayer would lurch, clanking and rattling, towards the potato drills, enveloped by a cloud of spray and a loudening hiss. The spray would flurry and whizz in Tommie's wake, running to rivulets as it stained the lank green stalks and the purple and yellow potato flowers.

After the spraying, my father would wheel each barrel on its rim back into place. The elbow of metal pipe that had broken in breaking his fall from the roof a few years before had never been replaced. As a consequence, a large yellow-green smudge marked the pebbledash where water from the remaining stump would splatter and gush freely into the barrel in wet weather. With Tommie's departure we could relax. My mother would hang her sodden apron on the clothesline and stand beside my father and say you must be tired after hauling all that water.

'Everyone behaved great,' he'd reply.

A summer came when he didn't bother to replace the barrels, but instead stepped back and forth where scutch grass and other weeds embroidered the rough, coarse-grained soil. I thought he must be reliving his fall but then he talked about sinking a chamber to store water and feeding a pipe into it from the house roof.

'Wouldn't an open pond be a danger?' my mother said. 'What would you do if one of the young lads fell in?'

'I'll seal it off under its own roof. I'll leave a gap to allow a bucket down and we can slide a cover over to keep everyone safe.'

'You and your elaborate plans,' she smiled.

Next day he began to dig. Surface clay and pebbles and grit were cleared. Then he came to an enormous boulder bedded amid the gravel. 'The only cure is to dig around it,' he said.

Still the boulder held fast, even defying a crowbar. He swung a sledge. Blow after blow made scarcely a dent. A mix of rain-smell and fire-smell spiked our nostrils as we looked on from a safe distance. Just as he was about to give up, a crack showed in the boulder. It widened with each succeeding strike. The interior of the boulder was dark blue. He used cold chisels, wedges and a pickaxe to claw the broken pieces free.

After a few days he had hacked down to a depth of seven or eight feet, covering a rectangular area of about twelve feet by ten. With ropes, Simon and I hauled our galvanised buckets half-filled with gravel and stones to the top. We dumped the debris in a hollow out where the nettles grew, swinging the heavy buckets as if they were thuribles even as they blistered our hands. We also helped mix concrete and my father smarmed the rough, steep sides of the chamber as far as the surface. Each time my mother called, all she had to talk to was the top of his begrimed head dipping and weaving as he trowelled. Only while idling in the Callows could I hope to forget myself the way work made him forget.

One morning I noticed a bubble forming in a corner of the chamber. The grey sludge-strewn ground glistened differently there, reminding me of the marl in the Callows glistening in its dampness. I heard a hissing note as if the earth was sighing, and then, to my surprise, a bubble detached itself and floated slowly towards me up through the chamber. I reached but it vanished before I could touch it. The hissing grew louder and was added to by a piping note quite similar to the song of the crickets that lived under Mattie's hob. A second bubble appeared, followed by a third and a fourth, a string of them issuing and some even making it away into the upper air.

'Water!' I shouted, scampering indoors.

'No more of your stories,' my mother said, but I urged her and my father out to see for themselves. The bubbles had stopped but now there was a definite trickling sound, and a tiny snake of water emerged, its clean, clear look becoming the colour of the sludge as it slid along.

'I own to God we've tapped into a spring,' my father said, and down the makeshift ladder he went to investigate further.

We could hear him dancing a sloppy jig. My mother immediately pronounced him stone-mad. By late evening the water had risen to a depth of one foot. He delicately stepped, not wanting to muddy the flow, and after skimming water into a cup he climbed the ladder one-handed and with great ceremony presented the cup to my mother.

'Ah, it's cold,' she breathed, after putting it to her lips. 'It tastes good.'

That was all the approval he needed. He worked late, hacking deeper and deeper in order to free the source. Over the next few days he roofed the well, using concrete which he reinforced with iron bars from the axles of broken horse-carts. The carts had been brought for repair by neighbours but never reclaimed as tractors increasingly took over from horses. He allowed an opening for a bucket, and an old tractor wheel served as a cover for the well until years later Vincent made a concrete lid with a metal handle sunk into it.

To my delight I got the job of clearing the last of the loose gravel from the wellhead because the access was too narrow for my father to fit through. He tied a rope about my waist and lowered me down. The stony smell was intoxicating and the cavern made my voice sound cold and strange. The water gurgled and hissed. I scooped a bucket into it, dredging the gravelly sludge as best I could. He raised the bucket by means of a rope. The bucket spun and dripped, spattering my face and hands. The water lapped about my wellington boots. Finally the loose debris was cleared. I fastened the rope about my waist and held tight while being hauled – a gasping gargoyle – to the surface.

Several times each day I checked the well. It rose steadily towards the surface. I dreamed it would overflow as the saucepan of porridge had done in an old fairy tale, but when I told Bridie about the dream, she said that no doubt both my father and the water knew what they were doing.

'I half-expected to find the spring all the time,' my father told us then, basking in my mother's smile. 'Doesn't it sit between the spring in Mullagh Beg and the one at Keaveney's well?'

He was claiming the well for himself, and this irritated me no end. I had got it into my head that the well was mine. I'd earned it and felt useful and watched over it and now ached to be given the credit from him in return.

'I realised that well was part of an underground stream such as you'll find in limestone places,' he big-talked. 'And, whatever about overflowing, it will never run dry.'

'Limestone water,' my mother agreed. 'It has such a cold kick it would leave you breathless after one gulp.'

'It's my well,' I blurted out.

'And why wouldn't it be?' he laughed. 'Hasn't it near enough of a gulp to accommodate the whole parish?'

He invited our neighbours to taste the water and draw their share. It saved them – and us – the walk to Keaveney's well. God, Larry, you're a diviner pure and simple, they enthused, but now the well belonged to everyone. Many conversations over many years would happen around it, casual as the gift of the water itself. And, once in a while, a quiet grumble aimed at us, its minders. Was there no way of stopping dust blowing in? Wouldn't you think a handier way of lifting could be devised? Our fussiest neighbour even got so precious he took to fretting that his enamel bucket would be damaged if he dropped it into the well. My mother listened politely and shook her fist in pretend anger behind him as he walked out the path. 'Let him stew in his juices,' she said before eventually placing on standby a galvanised bucket for his and everybody else's convenience.

I relinquished my sense of ownership – if slowly. The well itself saw to that. I could ask no better work than 'rising the water'. You held the bucket using both hands while making sure also to hold the looped rope in one hand so it had slack to accompany the bucket without impeding its upside-down entry. If you let go of the rope, as I sometimes did at the beginning, you would have to fish the bucket up by means of a long-handled crook borrowed from my father. If you threw incorrectly, the bucket would flop and float, refusing to fill. A loud thunk indicated an accurate hit. The play of the bucket plunging under would pleasure your wrists. The pressure came as you hauled up the wet rope, grip by grip, your palms burning by the time you'd landed the water glittering and splashing at your feet.

I knew the well was my father's from the beginning, of course. Only his stubbornness could make it produce, a sustained stubbornness becoming the order, and the genius, of his life. Still, I refused to let the well fully go. As I reached towards my teenage years I would begin to tap into a kind of defiance of my own and, as with the well, it never would dry up.

On a hot day without a breath of wind the hay we were saving began to stir and spin and take flight.

'Go on,' Pat Joe Treacy cried, dunting his pitchfork into the ground and furiously waving his arms above his head. 'Go and bring it all away. Take it with my blessing.'

And the unseen spirits or fairies – for it was these he addressed – spun the hay ever faster until a swathe of it lifted, flensing and wisping into the air. None of the men, not my father or any of the others, laughed at Pat Joe's remarks, but silently looked on until the brief flurry had abated. Did they, too, believe in the *séideán sí*? Or did they wish to play safe in case mocking was catching?

My brothers and I smiled behind their backs but we still wondered at the spectacle of the flying hay. We couldn't explain it, and a thing you couldn't explain, if sufficiently odd or awe-inspiring, might reasonably be called supernatural.

'O ye of little faith,' Father Keane said at Mass when the congregation rose as one for the Gospel, but in fact we overflowed with faith, taught to believe in a supreme and benevolent God and in an evil and, we hoped, lesssupreme Satan. But we also held to various homespun superstitions and would behave in ostensibly silly or irrational ways just to accommodate them.

Sometimes our foolishness – or our faith – seemed to work. When I was aged about twelve a wart grew on my thumb. I rooted at its tough fibres and managed to decapitate it, but it grew back, and several others grew to keep it company.

'Get an elderberry leaf and rub it on the warts,' Mrs Heagney said. 'Then bury the leaf, but don't tell anyone where you've buried it.'

I did as she instructed and within a few days the wild handful of warts had vanished.

My mother put her trust in the power of prayer. She said a supplication to St Anne which would, she believed, grant her not only the grace of a peaceful death but let her know of her impending death three days before it happened.

My father's way was to speak a word of blessing after felling a tree. Otherwise he took the weight off his mind by castigating what he saw as the injustices of the Church. Each Sunday while preparing for Mass, he would give his sermon – not that any of us paid particular attention as we rushed about to get ourselves ready, rummaging in the 'jail' under the staircase for shoes, shoe polish and socks that matched. Besides, his sermon was usually a repeat of the previous Sunday's. There he'd stand with galluses pushed off his shoulders and one leg up on a chair to keep his trousers from falling as he leaned in at the small smudged mirror placed on top of the television set. He shaved using soap and a cut-throat razor which he sharpened beforehand on a strop attached to a nail.

When the church needed funds for refurbishment, or when Father Keane 'promised' to read out the names and the amount paid or unpaid by each parishioner for Christmas or Easter dues, an extra whet was added to my father's sermon – this despite the fact that he and Father Keane remained always on friendly terms and that he would cheerfully repair altar rail or organ loft without remuneration.

'Princes of the Church,' he would begin. 'Imagine the luxury they live in, with their palaces and cathedrals and walled demesnes. What has that got to do with the teaching of Jesus? Did you ever see a thin bishop? Or a parish priest who didn't have the shine of soft living on him? And yet they have the gall to talk down to the rest of us. Would it not be more in their line to mind their own souls?'

'What about your own soul?' my mother would reproach.

'Oh, I'll leave that to God.'

Sermon terminated, my mother would help the white shirt over his broad shoulders and fasten the buttons – his fingers were too flattened from handling timber to manage the task on their own. A trace of soap or speck of blood might linger on his cheek despite his washing and towelling and, with extraordinary gentleness, she would lean in close to him and touch it away before placing his tie about his neck and fixing the knot.

'How do I look?'

'You look presentable.'

Mullagh Church was just a half-mile from our house. My father cycled; the rest of us walked. Father Keane was tall and stately and red-faced. He could be brusque or austere, but farm talk always loosened his tongue. He kept two racehorses – the only racing they did was around his fields, and sometimes they bit the rumps of his cattle. As a farmer he delighted in appearing shrewd. 'If they ask what price you got for your animals, tell them you did better than you expected but not as well as you had hoped.'

He seldom said much to us Mass-servers but stood with his back turned, whispering Latin prayers while vesting his priestly garments. The linen alb covering his own clothes he fastened tight at his midriff with the braided cincture. The cumbersome chasuble he worked over his head and about his shoulders. The amice with its small white cross he kissed. The long thin stole he slipped around his neck. The maniple, resembling a napkin, he draped daintily over his left forearm. I, in common with the other Mass-servers, fitted the inclined-to-rip surplice and soutane over my Sunday best, slugged from the bottle of altar wine before Father Keane arrived into the sacristy and – on his instruction – went out to swing from the belfry chain, all but levitating at the good of it as the iron

121

notes pealed across the fields, summoning our neighbours to the polished pews and the prayer-smell that the church seemed to hold and accentuate as it did even the least whisper.

Northwards from Foxhall, Castlenancy, Gurtymadden and Carrowshanbally the worshippers travelled, led by James Farrell driving a pony and trap. Southwards from Corbally, Carrowreagh and Poppyhill they drove or cycled. Eastwards from Finnure and Carrowntober and Corracurkia they moved, past Vincie Lyons's shop and the high, level hurling pitch. Westwards by Mullagh stream and the national school from as far as Gortnagappa and Gortavoher and Walshtown they journeyed. Only Mick Dillon of all the able-bodied stayed at home:

'Will we see you at Mass on Sunday, Michael?'

'You won't, priest, nor the Sunday after.'

I thought the remark funny but knew it took courage to say. Some of the men sat on kneelers at the back of the church and this didn't require courage, though their whispers occasionally reached as far as the altar. Other men stayed in the church porch, leaning their elbows on the stone baptismal font while they chatted. One or two were known to stand outside altogether, each with a hand placed against the church wall in the belief that this enabled them to remain connected with what was happening within.

'You men – come up. Come to the front. Come now,' Father Keane would call and beckon, every once in a blue moon.

Ignored, he would swoop from the altar. Heads would turn to follow him. Big men would shamble slowly forward with the priest assiduously moving them along. James Farrell, the only man who held a front-row pew, would lift from his devotions and remove the white hand-kerchief on which he knelt and move inwards to make room. None of the men ever got as far as his seat, how-ever. They each dodged, at the earliest opportunity, to a seat as far back as possible. Father Keane would ascend the altar steps and, after noisily blowing his nose into his – always plaid – handkerchief, would resume the Mass as though nothing had happened.

'Why do only boys serve Mass?' my sisters often asked.

'I don't know.'

'Why aren't women let in around the altar?'

'I couldn't tell you.'

I still served Mass, still enjoyed the sing-song of the Latin responses. Serving Mass during the week gave me licence to go on 'slow' bicycle races afterwards with my friend BP – our standard excuse after arriving to school an hour late being that 'the priest spent a long time talk-ing today'.

In the church, as at school, I longed to be outside. I tried to pray but the fervour with which I'd prayed as a young child now seemed defused. Sunshine shafting through the stained-glass windows became my idea of transfiguration. God was the grass and the trees and the wind blowing through them. God germinated out of the dust. God is still these things to me today. The concept of an all-powerful yet personalised God whom I might cajole or buttonhole for special favours doesn't attract me at all. Such a God would surely allow too many reasons to feel superior or disappointed, I tell myself.

As I grew older I could see everywhere about me how quickly the world would forget us. The seasons coming and going merged into one another, seeming to quicken year on year. Nature ate the dead. The inscriptions on their headstones became indecipherable, worn by rain and wind, frost and sun, blotched and gritted with moss and lichen. Even to step past the fallen gate near Lena Coyne's house, which was smothered by weeds and grass, was to be teased by the story of how a man and a woman leaning there to kiss had made it topple. But what their names were or how their love affair played out nobody could say. They were dead and gone and not even the mind of the seanchaí Jim Maguire could restore them.

'Maybe Mattie has the right idea,' I told myself. 'He does the first thing that comes into his head.'

He did follow certain routines, of course, such as calling once a fortnight to have my father cut his hair. 'There you are, Mary,' he would say to my mother, leaving a bundle of rhubarb sticks from his garden on the kitchen table. 'It'll make a good dessert.'

The barbering always took place on the path between house and workshop. Mattie would sit facing into the chair, his arms resting along its back and a towel thrown about his shoulders. He would draw down news of cattle bought or sold, or of how a neighbour might have come into a fortune or improved his house, or of a caper that someone – usually himself – had played. My father would make the odd harmless remark as he guided the trimmers around Mattie's speckled poll, but sooner or later he would fall into the trap of asking a question about one of the topics raised.

'Isn't it giving you great trouble?' Mattie would say, shuffling his shoulders. 'Wouldn't it be more in your line to mind your own business?'

'I was only asking . . .'

'And who are you to ask? You should never ask. Your opinion isn't called for. No one wants to hear what you think, good, bad or indifferent.'

The outburst, lasting for some minutes, always left me shaken. I willed my father to answer back or to walk away and leave the haircut unfinished, but he kept on trimming in silence, managing his older brother's giddy talking head as best he could. Mattie would rise suddenly, causing the legs of the chair to grate on the path, sweep the towel from his shoulders and shake it vehemently before stuffing it into his pocket and storming away home.

'He's as contrary as a bag of cats,' my father would say after taking the chair indoors.

'Aren't you worse for entertaining him?' my mother would respond.

'Ah, his nerves are at him.'

I'd sweep up the few scattered tufts of Mattie's hair and toss them into the fire, knowing that another row would rise two weeks later.

In certain respects I half-liked Mattie. Even his pride, what my mother called 'his fierce sense of high and mighty', was, if nothing else, good for a laugh. She never felt fond of him but she largely agreed with his idea that most people were 'too humble for their own good'.

'He makes a right circus of himself,' some neighbours criticised. 'He acts the gentleman, even though he has nothing to back it up with.'

'Aren't we the equal of anyone,' he would declare as if mindful of their opinion, 'and better than most?'

While still very young, Mattie had hit off for the Ford factory in Cork to buy a new car costing three hundred pounds. His parents promptly sent him back to recoup the money. He settled for an old jalopy and drove it through the war years when nobody else had a motor. He attended the Galway Races year on year and dreamed of owning a racehorse, but made do with a greyhound and wasn't bothered that it never won. He ferried the Mullagh senior hurling team to matches, three or four trips there and back each Sunday. He bid at auctions and brought back oil paintings and other items – a leech jar and an oriental parasol come to mind – from the last of the grandee houses around Ballinasloe; they lingered forgotten in shed corners. He hobnobbed with the 'big shots', gambling beyond his means, drinking when he was flush and going dry when funds were low.

But as time went by, I saw more clearly what my father meant. Mattie's nerves were at him. They must have bothered him even going back to the day in 1957 when he packed his suitcases with the intention of accompanying his brother Joe to America only to realise at the last moment that he couldn't go through with it.

'Wouldn't you think a smart man such as yourself would rebuild that fine gate pillar that's after collapsing in your haggard, Mattie?' a neighbour needled.

'I would if I thought I was going to live for ever.'

He relied on my father – for help with haymaking, for a chance to earn money doing odd jobs at the workshop, and of course for haircuts. It was as if he depended on him emotionally more than anything else, his every frustration vented safe in the knowledge that all would be borne calmly and without the need to retaliate.

About a week before the accident in Moore, he called in for a haircut. He mustered up his usual storm out of nothing, berating my father fiercely before heading homeward. But when news reached him of the death, he grew inconsolable, beating his fists against a wall and lamenting that he would never be able to speak a civil word to his brother again.

Mattie's health began to deteriorate some years later. He'd been talking amiably with us, asking my mother if there was anything she needed. He regarded himself as head of the family now more than ever, advising about the cattle and the hurleys and always inviting me to visit him before I returned to Dublin. One autumn, when the accumulated years had greyed and thinned his hair and accentuated the stoop of his back, he dabbed his hand in the little plastic holy-water cruet nailed above our porch door and ambled out saying 'Goodnight Mary, goodnight to ye all now'. Something made us follow him. He turned right, towards the Callows, instead of left to the boreen and along the old Mass path which led past Hough's house and through Shiel's land, his customary route.

'You're going the wrong way, Mattie.'

'How in Christ's name am I?'

'Go by the road; it's handier.'

'I will. I will.'

My mother and I chaperoned him on to the boreen and halfway along. 'I know where I am. Let me alone,' he insisted, and reluctantly we turned back.

Not that night but shortly after he fell into a well on a neighbour's land while trying to hoist a bucket of water. He struggled for a long time before dragging himself up, or being dragged up, to safety. He survived the ensuing cold but couldn't cope on his own any more. His brother Joe brought him to Dublin and cared for him but there came a point where he couldn't dress himself and he needed constant watching or he would wander out on to the streets.

Eventually he had to be placed in the care of the County Home in Loughrea, on the edge of the lake. At first he bemoaned his fate, saying the County Home was the last resort of paupers and beggars. Its facilities were in fact superior to those of most of the private nursing homes and, as time went by, Mattie found contentment there.

I visited him on a few occasions. Together we would stand at his window and he would lift and spread his hand towards the lake and the gentle hills of Aughty beyond. 'They're brooding,' he whispered to me once. 'The mountains are brooding. It's a sure sign of rain.'

His face held a shadow for a moment and then he jerked out his chin. 'Amn't I lucky all the same to have such a palace as this?' he confided. 'Many a man has to end his days in the County Home.'

After his death I did something which I hadn't dared to do while he was alive on account of his touchy nature. I went to see his gelignite well, blasted into the earth while British soldiers stood in attendance in 1919. A few bushes and a cairn of stones covered it. I dragged them back to reveal a perfectly rounded aperture and the gleam of water far below. I dropped in a pebble and after some seconds heard the splash. An image came to me – of thirst and forgetfulness – and I shaped a poem around it:

> Arragh himself, hollow with the drooth,
> certain that someplace a liquid coin
> stares up, is tunnelled, long way down.

Mattie's toing and froing was over. But then we uncovered letters he had received – closer to complaints than love letters – from a local woman who stated that she wouldn't marry him unless he built a modern house out on the main road, unless he stopped drinking, unless he got rid of that silly cap . . . We happened on those letters stuffed into the gable of his house, yellowed and weather-worn almost to disintegration, and after reading them we put them back. They'd mattered enough for him to keep them long after the romance was over, yet now they seemed of no more account than the rusty horseshoe placed alongside, or the sheep-dosing bottle that had turned green with the years, or the pair of crumpled, powdery shoes stuffed into a nearby nook.

I remembered a snippet of information I had found in *Reader's Digest* or some such magazine that Mattie had brought years before – about the 'holes of truth' into which, during the Middle Ages, the citizens of Florence would drop letters accusing other citizens of wrongdoing. Even Leonardo da Vinci had suffered in this way at the hands and pens of the 'do-gooders', finding himself ostracised because of his alleged involvement with another young man. Now the 'holes of truth' in Mattie's gable came to signify for me – in cahoots with the dust – the nature of oblivion, the wear and tear of the world, the end of things.

Storms came from the west, never seeming to learn new directions. The biggest storm of all arose when I was eight, and the man on the radio said the storm's name was Hurricane Debbie. Our whole house shook, and the chimney made a mournful sound that vowelled long and loud, unnerving us. The cypress trees stooped and groaned, gulping great mouthfuls of air and wrestling within the heavy, green-cloaked arms of themselves as if trying not to drown.

At a certain point my father hurried out and as soon came back minus his cap and called my mother from the door; then she ran to the haggard to help him stop the hay from blowing away. Frantically they tied down the hay-pikes using wire ropes weighted with stones at either end – some of the pikes had been left over from the previous year and the old straw ropes must have rotted or grown loose. Hurricane Debbie was determined to take every-thing, new or old. But my father slung up heavy tractor tyres and prevented the pikes from toppling by propping long planks of wood under them.

No sooner had he and my mother returned to the house than the electricity went, making the gasp of someone who has just been punched in the stomach, and we saw lightning stand a momentary but frenzied apparition at the two kitchen windows as if God had been tampering inexpertly with his fuse-boxes. Next moment the low rumble of thunder suggested to us now he is angry, now he is flinging furniture around the floor of heaven.

'Search in the jail for a candle,' my mother told me. I crept through the small door under the stairs and my hand identified the cold snout of a wellington boot and the even colder last that no one bothered to use for mending shoes any more, and then I could identify the candle less by its shape than by its shiny feel. When I emerged the sight of the black tubular lamp under the picture of the Sacred Heart made me think of Jesus quenched and I felt shocked at the thought.

Hurricane Debbie finally abated and the uprooted trees were cleared from the roads and the electricity was restored. My father resumed his visits *ar cuairt* to his friend Mick Dillon's candlelit house one or two nights a week to help pass the winter. Then, whether or not the absence of the electric light stirred nostalgia in them, or perhaps annoyed by the frequency with which the electricity would fail, some people began talking about how life had been simpler not so many years before, and regretting things that were gone, and saying that all the ghosts must have died since they depended on the darkness and the darkness had been electrocuted by the powerful electric light.

I didn't understand. As far as I could see there was still the dark night falling faithfully over us as the sun broke – the colour of egg-yolk on the horizon – and falling all the sooner if there happened to be no sunset, merely cloud or rain. There was still the Callows with no porch-light visible there, only will-o'-the-wisp carrying his cold flame. If all else failed, I reckoned there was still the *seanchaí*, Jim Maguire.

'God save all here, says the ghost of Jim Maguire,' I announced one evening on the way from school, mimicking the man himself.

'How in hell's blazes could Jim Maguire be the ghost?' my friend BP asked. 'Didn't I see him last night with his big brown woolpack of a corduroy trouser held up by the braces and his dinged hat on top of his head and his big laugh?'

'He is anyhow the ghost. In my mind he is.'

'You're cracked.'

'Take it back.'

'I will in my hole.'

We raised our fists and I swung one into his jaw. Just as sharply he caught me under the left eye. And there, with nobody to urge us on or drag us apart, we fought. BP's lips and teeth began to bleed but he wouldn't quit. We saw a neighbour's car approaching and agreed to break off until it passed. But as I lowered my guard, BP took advantage.

'Ah, he bet you,' my father said after seeing the black eye.

'You should see what I did to him. He's spouting blood.'

My father laughed and all I could do was go out to the ash-pit tree, the scabby old pine, and whisper the story into its sidelong branches.

'The damage is not how it looks to be,' he told my mother later, relating the story just as I had told it to the tree – no further proof needed in my mind that the ash-pit pine was enchanted.

Yes, BP and I squabbled over many things and shook hands afterwards and said 'peace'. But we came to blows over whether or not Jim Maguire was 'the ghost' and didn't speak to each other again until several days had elapsed. As for Jim Maguire, he visited while the long nights lingered, as he had done since before I was born.

'A stout man is a fine man,' my maternal grandmother, Molly Headd, often said, reflecting the opinion of the old people who had lived through the series of famines that had affected County Galway even into the second decade of the twentieth century. 'You would admire a stout man because he has provisions set aside for the hungry day coming over the hill.'

Jim Maguire's 'provisions' included his laugh. It would begin deep in his belly and work its way up, causing him to wiggle and tickle his underarms as if facilitating its journey.

He smoked a pipe, and I noted my mother's frown each time he spat on the floor. We would be allowed to stay up late to listen to his stories. Usually when there were visitors we stood with our backs to the wall, or we sat on the form well away from the fire. This deference to the big people was expected. They spoke to each other and we listened in silence. On the rare occasions they spoke to us, we gave a 'yes' or 'no' answer. If we whispered among ourselves we were told to stop making noise or were asked if we wanted to go into another room. That was the way, our otherwise fair and reasonable parents as strict in this matter as their neighbours and as the old-fashioned times they lived in.

Sometimes Jim's stories passed over our heads, but we tolerated them just so we could laugh at his laugh, hide our laughs behind it, even mimic it as we grew older and became smart-alecky. His laugh would emerge as a high-pitched wheeze, and when he could no longer control the wheeze, he threw back his head and slapped his thighs and unleashed such beasts of mirth as made the crockery on the dresser shake.

My parents enjoyed him to such an extent that the clock was forgotten and our bedtime indefinitely postponed. Years would pass before I understood how Jim's stories had enriched us. Stories that now – more even than at the moment of their telling – seem ghosts. Ghosts of dead people, the mischief they got up to and the witty remarks they made. Ghosts of rivers that the county council had begun dredging and of forts they were running trunk roads through because we needed modernity and a practical purpose should attach to everything. Ghost of the Bishop's Chair in Morgan's field which had been a Mass rock in Penal times, and ghost of the 'hungry sod' which, if you happened to step on it, might send you astray for hours even in your own field. Ghosts of place-names whose Gaelic names helped to remember their original topography or the happenings associated with them before they were given a linguistic twist, so we knew only to speak them crookedly in the end. Ghost of the Kiltulla Ash where van Ginkel stopped to shelter from a rainstorm after the Battle of Aughrim, and ghost of the Duniry Ash – huge and hollow – used as a house by a weaver and his family before it was made to serve as a children's classroom. Ghosts of harrow and plough, of scuffle and hay plotter, and ghosts of horses – including Jim Maguire's own – that pulled them, together with ghosts of cows and pigs and hens and geese and pheasants and foxes and hares and badgers all mingling in the menagerie of the storyteller's wheeze and freed again in his raucous laugh. Ghosts of native grasses and herbal cures and summer flowers – these were the ghosts Jim Maguire kept alive even in dead of winter to amuse and enlighten, caution and embolden those who had the wit to take them in.

We became our own stories, our own seasons and our own place – the truest of celebrities – by virtue of the tales the *seanchaí* told; we conversed again with people who were dead.

'The ghosts are dying out,' Jim announced one night. 'And if they are, it's all down to the power of the electricity.'

In a way he was proved right. We plagued and pestered my mother until she bought us a television set. She and my father seemed to listen rather than watch, just as we would watch rather than listen, especially when *Top of the Pops* and the first music videos came on. 'Push back,' we were advised, 'or it'll burn holes in your eyes.'

Sometimes the screen would show a blizzard, or the picture would move slowly, repeatedly upwards or downwards, or flip at high speed, or go horizontally berserk. Other hazards included the high-noon scene in the western getting pulled asunder, the car chase becoming wrecked, the close-up of a face blobbed or squashed into a phantasm such as had happened to my own reflection once in the ripples of Keaveney's well.

The news demanded silence. The weatherman was often scolded. Guests on talk-shows were praised, cajoled or castigated right to their goggle-box faces. We youngsters dreamed of being American because in America the sun shone all the time and the good guys could get away with murder if it was done for the right reasons. Our copycat metallic-silver guns fired noisy caps and our sally-rod arrows whizzed from the purplish-brown bows we had stripped from the shoulders of the cypresses. And when a tapping came to the door one evening and Jim Maguire walked in, we didn't at first realise he was there. Then the television light shivered against his face and we caught him blinking as he back-tracked from the kitchen, never to return.

'What would you say to a river that rises just twenty-four miles from the sea,' the Master asked one day while in a good mood, 'and then turns its back on the sea and heads off southwards for two hundred and forty miles before meeting up with the sea?'

'I'd say it has the notions of being a big river,' BP, sitting in a casual sprawl beside me, said. 'And what's more, you're talking about the River Shannon.'

'Two answers and both of them right,' the Master chuckled. 'Saints preserve us, will wonders never cease? But would you ever sit up and put your feet under you like a good young lad?'

Then he pointed at the big frog-green map alive with clusters of little blue eyelets and said Ireland resembled a saucer in that it had a more or less flat middle with mountains around the edges. Rivers would follow the natural gradient in order to get to the sea. The Shannon, which was named after a goddess, was Ireland's longest river because she dragged her heels over the flat plains and dawdled in certain low-lying places, and that's how her three big lakes came to be formed.

'The Shannon is no goddess to the farmers,' he told us then. 'She's more of a lazybones to them, just as you lot here before me are lazyboneses now.'

We laughed obligingly, and he talked on about how the Shannon didn't properly do her job of draining the land. Rather, she sometimes overspilled her banks, and that's how the big Callows that lay between Athlone and Portumna came to exist.

'We have our own Callows,' I said up to him, unable to contain myself.

'Your own Callows?' he queried, tightening his jaw. 'How is that the case?'

'Up the fields,' I said.

'Ah, you're mistaken,' he said. 'That's not a Callows. The word "Callows" comes from "*caladh*", an Irish word meaning "river meadow". You're talking about a miserable old bit of marshy ground, or maybe a cutaway bog.'

I wanted to tell him about how our Callows might be very small, not like the great Shannon Callows, and how she might be nothing special to look at – dull brown in colour because of the rushes and flaggards growing abundantly in patches – but she was still a Callows because she owed her existence to rivers. Her four rivers might be very small compared to the great goddess of the Shannon, but still they flooded sometimes, even if often as not they stagnated. I wanted to mention how her grey pools reflected clouds that you would be inclined to think would hang overhead for ever, and how she had hidden quagmires that could swallow a beast, and one whirlpool with algal edges green and calm.

So much I wanted to say about her flowers and birds, too, but I dared not. One glance at the vein beating on the side of the Master's face told me that his mood was changing back, and I didn't want to be responsible. For when he changed, everybody suffered. At such times the girls were referred to as 'dishwashers' and the boys as 'turnip-snaggers', fit only for the scullery and the sodden fields. 'There's a big world out there!' he would shout, spinning the tin globe noisily on its axis between his upraised hands. 'A modern, changing world, and how in heaven's name can I be expected to equip you ignoramuses for it if all you are able to do is speak Bog English, the language of muck savages?'

The best policy in his classroom was to keep your mouth shut, though this might leave the flurry of enthusiasm in your heart disappointed. If picked, you couldn't easily avoid reading a passage from a book or attempting an answer, but you said the words our way first – broadening the vowels and slurring some consonants – maybe to put the Master to the trouble of checking you, but more because our way felt right, the natural way for us. It came with our place and the accent of our place, even with a sprinkle or twist of the Old Irish that our great-grandparents had spoken, which we still used in our everyday lives without thinking about it.

The schoolyard had its own lessons to teach, and some of them were every bit as harsh as the Master's. You had to act tough or certain other lads would go through you for a short cut. So I said as little as possible, and though

I wanted to rev the motor inside me up to full throttle, I walked with my hands dug to the elbows in my trouser pockets, and pretended to be unimpressed about everything. But the Master, by favouring me in class, kept complicating things as far as a peaceful life in the yard was concerned. 'Tell them, Pat,' he would say and, though I felt bad about it, I gave him the answer he wanted.

'Tell them, Pat,' someone would shout in the yard, pushing in on me.

'It's not my fault if you happen to be a thickhead.'

'Are you looking for a fight?'

'I am if you are.'

'You're afraid of your shite.'

Within seconds a human circle would form, prodding and goading until words turned to blows.

I exulted in the fight. It made me feel more alive even than sprinting barefoot in the Callows could. It killed the sadness. Other boys found my left-handedness awkward to handle. I didn't cry, nor did my face easily cut or bleed. Crying or bleeding could stop a fight, and sometimes I was relieved that my rival cried or bled because this proclaimed me the winner when I knew in my heart that I had lost.

Being chaired by your friends around the concrete yard after a fight was as good as winning a trophy in a hurling match. Making up with the other boy and accompanying him to the stream that ran by the hurling field to wash the blood from his face served as well to wash away my own hurt and to make me feel good-natured again.

The more we got things 'wrong', the more the Master insisted on proper grammar. One evening he summoned a group of children to the front of the class. There they waited in line. His cane swished through the air and down hard on the first boy's palm. The hand seemed to wither under the blow, its owner momentarily buckling in on himself before dancing sideways in a spasm of pain. Two more slaps, then it was the other hand, with again the swish and crack and the boy twisting now in the opposite direction. Everybody in the row received six of the best.

'Get out of my sight,' he said then, and they slouched back to their desks, some of the boys brazen-faced, others pressing their palms against their bellies or folding them under their oxters, tears shining in the girls' eyes.

'Tell them, Pat.'

I dug my nails into the top of my desk and didn't speak.

'Tell them, Pat,' he repeated.

Getting the answer right and hearing the Master's praise had often kept me going, but now I looked at him and did what I hadn't done since my first year at school – I shrugged. Back then, this habit often irritated the teacher. On one occasion, she lost patience and slapped me. I was hoping for the same result now from the Master. He waited a long while, the vein at the side of his temple pulsing as his jaw clenched and unclenched. It was a game between us, but no matter what else might happen, all I had to do was sit tight, stay silent.

At last he moved to the tall windows and stood gazing out at the stream and the half-built bungalow across the road. He put his hands in his pockets and kept his back towards us. The silence deepened. The pale distempered walls with their huge dog-eared maps, the chart listing its eleven irregular Irish verbs, the stack of hard-cover books gathering dust on shelves, the porcelain inkwells set into the oak desks, the Sacred Heart lamp and the empty fireplace, even the blackboard with its long lines of chalked grammar, all seemed swallowed up by the welling silence, but I told myself it didn't matter. This was an adult game and I had won.

There were consequences, of course. Over the following weeks and months, the Master became stand-offish towards me, praised my work less, and directed his questions elsewhere. I felt caught in a bind, desperate for his approval while yet not wanting to be set apart or spared the treatment handed out to other boys and girls. Finally, after my brother Simon had been slapped for no reason that I could discern, I staged a silent protest, leaving my books unopened on the desk. The Master ignored me for a long time and then, of a sudden, he was at my shoulder.

'Are we now to understand that you are on strike?'

He hauled me from the classroom and down to the sally trees growing in and beside the stream. There was a water-lapped stone near the sturdiest of them.

'Jump on to it,' he said.

I jumped and slipped, wetting my shoes.

'That one,' he said, asking me to break off the thickest sally rod. 'I don't know what's got into you but, by God, I'll knock it out.'

Back to the classroom we marched. Three of the best laced on to either hand, and through the cutting pain I felt justified, treated the same as everybody else at last.

The days dragged. Near the end of our time in Sixth Class we learned from the Master that he was soon to retire. He wished us well and said that while he realised he had been very severe on us, he'd intended it only for our good and he hoped there were no hard feelings.

The classroom was crowded on his retirement day owing to the fact that many of the younger children had been ushered in to help give him a good send-off. 'I brought you all some sweets,' he said, taking a fancy tin box from the cabinet built into the side-wall and placing it on his desk. But then he got into a confab with another teacher and we grew increasingly noisy. He warned us to be quiet but we were thinking only of the sweets.

'Very well, if that's the way you want it,' he shouted finally. 'There won't be any sweets.'

He grabbed the box and chucked it back into the wall cabinet and slammed the door shut. The Sacred Heart lamp above it flickered and tottered for a long moment before crashing from its pedestal and shattering on the classroom floor.

I found myself adrift for several months in Seventh Class – whatever the cause of the delay in moving to secondary school, I am unable to recall it now. The new Master didn't accuse us of Bog English or call us disparaging names but he could be just as strict as his predecessor. He had more modern ideas, however. He asked me to help another pupil whom some of the boys said was 'retarded'. I enjoyed working with this boy and his happiness at getting a sum right or reading a sentence seemed more and more to become my own. And though I didn't recognise it at the time, maybe my desire to work as a teacher had its beginnings there.

'It's a damnable thing, Jeemie,' Mattie said, caught in a reverie of regret as he drove us home from Kenny Park in Athenry where our parish senior hurling team had just played Turloughmore in the 1966 county final. 'It's a damnable thing but they lost it.'

At each bend in the road he would repeat this, and with each change of gear he would rock gently back and forth. His friend Jimmy Hough, Paddy Joe's cousin, who occupied the front passenger seat and who consoled himself by dragging continuously on a cigarette, agreed that, sure, it was a damnable thing. And when I eyed my father, wedged beside me in the cramped back of the car, he slowly shook his head and looked downcast, for while Turloughmore were winning their sixth championship in a row, we had no senior title to show since the 1930s.

Defeat or not, that was the day when, just turned thirteen, I fell in love with hurling as a spectacle. I can still remember specific incidents from the match – a diving save across the goalmouth by Seán Broderick, the dust rising as he braved the flying hurleys and pounding feet of the Turloughmore forwards; a long-distance free by Pakie Cahalan that swerved and dipped until the sliotar and the sunlight danced together high in the roof of the net; and, as Turloughmore fought back to win, the hand of Paddy Fahy dismissing a swathe of blood from his forehead casually as another man might discard his cap.

Hurling had begun for me with games against my brothers, resulting in frequent rows over whether the sliotar had travelled inside or outside the coats that served as our makeshift goalposts. On Sundays Simon and I would cross the fields to Cahalan's house, to hurl against Mikie and Stephen, or they would visit us.

At school, hurling would become one of the few games we played with any seriousness. In fact for a long time it seemed the only game in existence apart from Gaelic football. I remember several of us looking on in surprise some time in the mid-1960s as Dickie Rock and members of the Miami Showband played an impromptu soccer match on the hurling pitch before their gig at the local dance carnival – we were agog not because this was a 'foreign' game banned by the GAA but because we had never seen soccer played live before.

The Master would organise lifts for us to compete against schools from Carrabane, Woodford, Kilconieron and Kiltormer, and we would eventually 'graduate' to play on Mullagh club underage teams, a clutch of us crowded into the back of a car with our friend TJ afforded just enough elbow room to manoeuvre his accordion as he sang 'Streets of Baltimore' by way of shortening the journey.

Though facilities at Mullagh – apart from a good field – were lacking, we trained on two or three evenings each week, often staying until nightfall or even beyond. Some of the hurlers had Sétanta's own skill, and they would go on to star with the county team. On the big lawn outside his house where we sometimes practised, I saw Iggy Clarke puck a sliotar twenty times high into the air without catching it or letting it touch the ground, and without moving from the spot where he stood. When he tried to show me, I managed four or five pucks but after each one I would have to scamper forward to be under the dropping ball.

Initially I was given the dubious honour of minding goal. I consoled myself that, even if I might not save much, I had the guarantee of hanging the sliotar out after every score or wide ball. There were no nets and I dreaded especially to see Andy Cahalan – a most gentle person otherwise – charging through, for he would lash the sliotar a good fifty or sixty yards past, necessitating a dash on my part to find and retrieve it from the long grass behind the posts.

When I got to play outfield, I scrambled the odd goal and received an occasional knock of a hurl across the knuckles or the knee. These small scars of battle would remain, and be augmented by others later. Often I found I wasn't quick enough or possessed of the requisite handiness, but in hurling the rap had to be taken whether you got there first or not, and no remarks passed.

Later, long after I had given up playing, I would attend matches at Croke Park, including the All-Ireland final of 1980 when Galway finally made the breakthrough by defeating Limerick. I remember scampering, in tandem with Judy and throngs of other people, over the wire fence at the Canal End and on to the pitch to celebrate. There would never be a wet day again in our lives, so we imagined; and then I thought of my father, how the victory had happened just too late for him, and even as I laughed and cheered the tears played puck with my eyes.

One night at Mullagh a tinker boy started hanging around. He had been warned to clear off by a few of the older lads earlier, to clear off to hell. They must have thought he was trying to rob something from our clothes which we'd left by the side of the ditch when we togged out. He moved away a bit, back from the sideline, and everyone forgot about him, but now here he was again, looking at us and listening to our talk as we togged off.

'Fierce fine weather altogether,' he said.

'Show that animal the gate if he can't find it for himself,' a big fellow said, nudging me in the ribs.

I looked at the boy's thin begrimed face, at his ragged clothes and the 'iroch' or band of rash about the calves of his legs, and something softened in me and I heard myself say no, he has the same right as any of us to be here.

'Go on, I defy ya, give him a good flake.'

'He didn't do anything to me.'

'Ah, you're pure fuckin' useless.'

He lifted the tinker by the throat and flung him heavily on to the ground. The boy got up and without a word walked away from us. I wanted to follow him, to say that I was sorry for what was done. But instead I stooped to untie my bootlaces and tug off the heavy socks, and felt almost grateful for the sudden, sharp sting of the dew-dampened grass where the hard leather had caused my toes to chafe.

The incident with the traveller lad would come back to me at odd moments for years afterwards, provoking each time a quiet heart-scald. My lack of response to the way he was treated provided a lesson I would try to draw on in my dealings with children when I became a teacher: do the right thing, speak out against prejudice.

Usually after hurling practice I would stop to chat or buy refreshments at Owenie's shop, where a gaggle of us would toss our bicycles in a tangled heap, but on the evening in question I headed home, turning off the main road towards Mullagh Beg with the intention of herding the cattle, as my mother had asked me to do. I stood on the second-from-top beam of the big wooden gate near the end of the boreen and looked in. The fields, recently divided among local small farmers by the Land Commission, were fenced distinctively from the stone-wall or clay-rampart style common to the area. The stakes were of concrete, with six taut strands of thorny wire running between them – an effective means of keeping the animals from trespassing, even if the lack of trees and hedges did lend a certain featurelessness or absence of definition to each field.

There were, however, a few clumps of furze growing in the hollow between our two fields, and among them I could see the cattle bedded down for the night. I should have done a head count and the usual check – healthy cattle chewed the cud while resting and stretched them-selves when made to stand up – but on this occasion, feeling distracted or dispirited by the earlier episode at the hurling pitch, I did not.

The worry – and a bad conscience – gnawed at me as I cycled the remainder of the journey home. Next day a neighbour brought news that one of our prime bullocks was dead. His front fetlock had become caught in the forked branch of a blackthorn, and it bothered me greatly to think of how he had lain there all night unable to extricate himself.

My parents didn't say much after the initial recrimin-ations abated. They must have seen how miserable I felt. We loaded the big bloated carcass on to the forklift and it was given to me to drive the tractor slowly home so

the burnhouse lorry could collect the animal for rendering into meat and bonemeal. For a long time afterwards
the games of 'if only' wheeled in my head. But what hurt
more keenly was seeing the extra work my parents took
on as they tried to ensure that we wouldn't go short, to
make good the loss for which I was responsible.

'You're choking the hammer,' my father said when I failed
to drive the nail straight. 'Hold it further back along
the handle. Now hit, hit the nail on the head. There's a
rhythm to it. You'll know you've hit it right by the sound
it sends back.'

I didn't know. I might know all kinds of stuff that could
be found in books, such as the idea that it took human
beings one million years to learn how to grip a cudgel and
one million more to swing it so it landed flat on the work,
but this didn't seem of much use when I myself hadn't
mastered the knack.

'Go with the grain,' he said, showing us how to handle
smoothing plane and spokeshave. It had to do with process,
or precision of process, but the fact that each article was
hand-finished meant that it stayed a tiny fraction short
of machine-won finesse, and this actually helped to
individualise and endear it to the potential customer. My
father found examples of the various maladies in wood
– the grain might have spirals or piths or growth-breaks
in it, or even 'heart shakes'– and these were best excluded
right at the start.

'You have to get your eye in,' he said, lifting an ash
plank on to the bench and placing a hurley on top of it to

serve as a pattern. 'Now show me how you would mark that.'

I marked with my pencil along the contours of the pattern, knowing enough to avoid the knot that might enhance the look of a tabletop but was guaranteed to spoil a hurley.

'See the way the grain curves here,' he said, his hand running along the plank to where it widened into what would become the *bas*. 'Make sure to catch that curve. If you don't, your hurl will break at the first clash. Doing is the best way to learn. Maybe sometimes it's the only way.'

We picked up from his example. At least my brothers did. Simon learned how machines could be humoured, tools manipulated and gadgets mended. He became an expert hurley maker. Vincent, while still very young, surprised us with his talent for fixing electrical appliances. One night when the wireless went dead, he took it apart and, though a few pieces were left over after he had put it back together, a display light came on behind the little red rooster at the start of the waveband and the familiar smell of warm dust rose from the cabinet and the cheerful voice of Larry Gogan filled the kitchen.

New uses for old things – these were what my father and his brothers had always looked for, and the same now applied. Vincent used the gearbox of an old Morris Minor to move the carriage of the sawmill, a real labour-saver. And when a neighbour's washing machine gave up the ghost, he adjusted its motor and drum to operate the emery belt driven by the sander.

I tried to match my brothers – it wasn't laziness that held me back. I even enjoyed the more basic jobs such as lifting and chopping and hauling, but felt at cross-purposes with every knacky implement.

'Can you show him, Simon?' my father said after I'd messed up while planing a hurley one evening. Hearing this, I planed crazily and the blade became snagged with shavings. Simon spent several minutes taking the plane apart just to make it workable again.

On another occasion I planed until the handle of the hurley had become too thin. 'That's good for nothing now only the fire,' my father said. 'Run your eye along the hurl as you plane. It's better to leave it proud than to go too severe. Remember the timber can never be put back.'

'My eye is out,' I would say, throwing his language back at him. Or, 'I have a heavy hand.'

He still tried to make me into a carpenter even while shaking his head at my lack of aptitude. I could admire the rhythm of his work and, because he tried to coax rather than browbeat, I wanted to emulate the 'rightness' of his craft skills, to please him and earn his approval. But my clumsiness and an increasing lack of interest got in the way. I shrugged and shirked, feeling that I was going against the grain of my own make-up.

The relish with which he spoke – the terminology he used seeming almost to become the task itself – would nonetheless offer a hint as to how I might proceed later on when I started writing poems. Old-minted expressions that had been handed down through generations of hewers and shapers – 'the truth of the square', 'the sighting of the wood', 'the well of the bench', 'the throat of the bandsaw', 'the temper of the blade' – came back to me not just as belonging to him but as sounding *poetic*.

'You will need to smarten up,' my mother said. 'You're bright at the books and you would be well able for secondary school if it could be afforded.'

I thought of her as being on my side, pleased with my success at school. There, my awkwardness hadn't mattered. While my brothers considered sawmill and workshop as an escape from school, for me things worked the other way around. Where their talent lay in the ability to make and mend and to enjoy – tough though the job might be – handling implements or figuring out how they worked, my talent for book-learning seemed, in spite of my mother's encouragements, a less valued or valuable attribute.

'Jig-acting' was the expression my father used to describe my giddiness. But the more he and my mother asked me to stop, the more reckless I became. One afternoon during the threshing I accidentally stabbed Simon in the leg with a pitchfork while we were both chasing a rat that had emerged from a stack of oats. On another occasion I dislocated Ena's collarbone by pulling her from the little loft above the wardrobe upstairs during a game of hide-and-seek. I remember being terrified when she fainted, and all my protestations about not meaning to hurt her didn't change the fact that she had to be taken to hospital.

Some of the injuries I inflicted on myself weren't accidental, however. They came about following rows with my father. He'd find fault with my work and I would stare at him, full of hatred, then storm off to one of my 'places' to nurture my sense of grievance. I'd imagine him laughing at me and this would keep the rage burning for a while. Finally, hunger would begin to bite and I'd skulk homeward, feeling foolish but anguished still. In our old ramshackle shed at Mullagh Beg I found another way of coping. I put my fingers into a beehive under a mat of hay and the stings I received brought a peculiar solace. Then, after another argument, I ran barefoot through a patch of nettles until my toes – already damaged from wearing shoes that were too tight – grew badly seared and swollen.

'Aren't you the clever man?' he said. 'If you're so smart, why do you keep bringing trouble into the house and causing hurt to yourself?'

I shouted back at him and swung my fist, but he grabbed me by the arms and threw me across the kitchen. I landed backside first against the door of the 'jail' under the stairs, a soft landing, but my humiliation burned and I ran out into the darkness. It was bitingly cold but I couldn't show weakness so I stayed gone all night, lying on the boards of the trailer and feeling the nettle-scald in my feet and looking up at the thousands of stars twinkling heedlessly.

'Come in, can't you?' my mother pleaded, unable to find me because I had covered myself with a bundle of straw. 'He won't say a word. You shouldn't have vexed him. Please come in.'

I spent the night there, shivering, imagining things in the stirrings of the hawthorn bushes behind me and leaning on my elbow, hoping my father would appear suddenly and say he understood it all – my awkwardness, my upset, my difference from him.

The smallest details of that night and the following day stay with me – the feeling of stiffness and cramp, the itch on my skin, the sky greying for dawn that got me walking, the dew beginning to glisten on the grassy fields, the spider's webs hanging loosely along bushes and fence-posts. I remember seeing a herd of cows lying in the shelter of a tree, their big mournful eyes looking at me without wonder. I climbed the high, taut strands of thorny wire strung between concrete posts at the Land Commission fields and nudged under a furze clump for shelter. My stomach grumbled, and about me the breeze whistled among the furze thorns until the entire bush shivered and sprang – this way, that, on its two bandy legs. I had the feeling of waiting, endless waiting. I longed to be able to eavesdrop on my home. Was my father regretful? Did my mother cry? Were they searching for me now? The wind murmured. The furze creaked. I shifted position and put my hand back and suddenly my wrist was enclosed by a tightening silver loop of thin wire fixed close to the ground, a rabbit snare that had been set into place and made to hover there – a 'halo' – above a burrow. I ripped the snare from the burrow mouth, and untangled it from my wrist, and that was good enough to change my mind and send me home.

I still wonder at the child I was and the way I behaved. Not that I didn't know which end of me touched the ground, as my father had suggested; more that I couldn't seem to determine where I ended and everything else began. The world set limits and it bumped and bruised and bloodied me because I didn't keep to them. It knocked my rough edges off, as my father said it would. I would learn kindness yet, or the kindness in me would emerge, but as to how he or my mother reacted to my staying out all night I have no recollection. I only know that the escapade didn't leave me any the wiser.

A short time later, but without a row having happened, I rolled up my shirt cuffs and dragged first my left wrist, then my right, across a strand of thorny wire fencing. The stinging sensation seemed to lift the anguish from my mind and I grew calm behind my panic at the steadily trickling blood and the big white cuffs flopping down over my wrists but failing to hide or to stop anything.

'Are you trying to maim yourself?' my mother asked. 'Haven't you a good home? Isn't everything provided for you? Do you not see the harm you are doing?'

I stayed tight-lipped, felt glad of her attention and guilty at how my behaviour was making her sad. I remembered my father dancing on top of the chimney wall. His game, intended to get her to say she loved him, had seemed to take on its own dangerous momentum. He'd needed reassurance after their row, and maybe the lack I felt was similarly driving me now. I thought of how I had defied the Master. That triumph was wearing thin. I felt muddled, out of step. 'Swallowing dictionaries', 'gaping at nothing' and 'roaming' the Callows weren't part of what was required for survival in the real world. I wondered how I might manage or what, for that matter, was my world.

In the space of the year that followed, my unruliness persisted, resulting in many mishaps, including a number of dislocated bones and other injuries. After each mishap I was taken to Tomsie Irwin's house in Lurganmore. Tomsie had the gift of bone-setting, which, though it went back to before the time of Hippocrates, was seen as 'doubtful' by conventional medical practitioners. My parents, however, in common with most country people, had no doubt: Tomsie, the 'man of the healing hands', would see you right. He sits low-sized in my memory, and stern in the way that only his sternness could right the bone. No anaesthetic and no plaster. Yet gentle still.

'A penny will do,' Tomsie would say after fixing me up, but my father would give him a ten-shilling note. Its robin-redbreast colour made me feel guilty as Tomsie agreed to take it on condition that, in keeping with his own deed, it was 'in the spirit of a gift'.

Then I fractured my big toe when an oafish corner-back stomped on it during a hurling match. Shortly after I had recovered from that I hurt my left knee in a reck-less jump from a high ditch. The pain engulfed me, the sharp jab when I tried to put my foot on the ground left me faint. I hopped home on one foot and rested up for three days. The knee grew more swollen, the pain more severe. Again I was taken to Tomsie's house. 'Ye might as well head away now,' Tomsie told my father and Mattie, who had given us a lift. 'This job might take a while.'

Carefully he stretched and twisted the knee, trying to free the bone of constricting muscles in order to restore it to its proper position. I stared at the smoke-yellowed ceiling and silently implored the pain to stop. Finally he held the leg at a certain angle and applied his thumbs with controlled force to a point towards the inner side of the knee. I felt the bone move excruciatingly back into place.

It was a stormy night and he put me on the back of his old Honda motorbike where I clung on, feeling every bump in the road as we headed downhill, dispensing noise and smoke in equal abundance, towards home. He carried me past the madly writhing shapes of the cypress trees and into my parents' house. I mumbled thanks but he said the best thanks might be to 'study' myself in future and I told him I would try to do that.

Each of my recuperations lasted a week, sometimes two. I spent my days by the range, reading schoolbooks or, when the chance arose, full-colour Marvel comics which my mother had bought in Duffy's or in Kelly the Printer's in Loughrea. Spiderman would swoop from skyscrapers to ensnare super-villains, the Mighty Thor would give Mjolnir, his famous lump hammer, a swing, and Doctor Strange would prevail over evil sorcerers in mystic lands by means of his glowing amulet; but I was an invalid and not a bit in the world anyone could do about it.

My mother never once scolded me. In fact she couldn't do enough to ensure my comfort – a cushion, a footstool, a stick to lean on – but I took it all as my due. Sometimes she would stop off from her work to tell me stories. I recognised when a story was coming by her habit of taking one step to her right, there on the kitchen floor, before beginning, but, though I found this curious, I said nothing.

During this time the stories often had to do with me. A story about the hay-saving July day when, heavily pregnant, she had been brought to hospital by Mattie in his car and how her awkwardness around him caused the contractions to stop and my birth to be delayed. A story about how, on seeing me stand up for the first time, she let the plate she was carrying fly from her hands. A story about the morning when, aged two, I got a bad pain in my stomach and she feared I was going to die.

We both laughed at the stories, but when she told me

about her hope that I might attend secondary school – an opening available to very few during her childhood – her eyes misted over and I thought it must be on account of the grief I had caused, but no, she said, it didn't have anything to do with that at all.

And then she told me about her own early life, signalling that a story was imminent by taking that one sideways step. Or she would recite a poem from her schooldays, or a composition she had written. 'Most of the time,' she said, 'I was busy with the farming. I couldn't have asked for better work. Once a week I'd go by horse and cart to buy groceries for my parents. Ballinasloe was nine miles distant. The barge lorry would bring flour and tea and sugar, as well as animal foodstuffs to the yards at the backs of the shops, and I'd fill my cart. I didn't enjoy the lifting, but then I was only twelve.'

She gave me ballads written by her mother, who in her own childhood had heard the last of the wandering bards. One of Molly Headd's poems was about her son and my Uncle Lawrence, the village blacksmith in Killoran. Reading it, I saw the value of poets and artists of all descriptions. Without them the memory of things would fade, and there would be no proper celebration of the makers and the shapers, or indeed no mention of 'Felix Randal' in the poem by Hopkins or of how he 'Didst fettle for the great grey drayhorse his bright and battering sandal!'

Another Felix, the renowned uilleann piper Felix Doran, had often visited Killoran during my mother's childhood. 'His music did us a power of good,' she said. 'It was sunshine for the hay but it could also be the rain.

Whether or which, his playing could make the worry slip from a person's face and the work fall from their hands.'

She talked of the yarns swapped through the years with her sister Freda – being the two youngest of nine children and the only two girls, they were 'very great'. And of the wedding ring – it looked too tight on her finger – which she and my father had chosen at Faller's jewellery shop in Ballinasloe. 'The wedding breakfast took place in Hayden's Hotel. It was harmless enough; cold meats, tea and bread, and we had thirty guests. Mattie, the driver, couldn't be found in time to get us to the train for our honeymoon in Jurys in Dublin, so we decided to stay in a guesthouse in Galway city instead.'

Bonfires lit their return. And – a lovely, bygone custom – sods of turf dipped in paraffin and set ablaze by neighbours were carried as torches in procession through the darkness to lead them into their house.

My favourite of her stories had to do with the owl she caught while footing turf with my father during their early married days and the romance of swinging it gently home in a canvas bag between them – 'a ghost even to itself'. She told me that over the following years she had occasionally thought of the owl, and wished for it back, but then agreed it would probably escape up the chimney exactly as it had done before.

'Foolishness,' she would say, taking another step, this time to her left, and now I saw what the steps signified – she was skipping out of the practical roles of mother, housewife and farmer and into the notional and imaginative worlds of her secret self, then back again.

Years later, after I had settled in Dublin, we kept in

touch by letter and, as she grew old, more and more by phone. Our conversations dwindled – an hour, a half-hour, a bare ten minutes by the time she was in her seventies. One day I got a phone call from her. The line was poor and her voice low.

'I love you,' she said.

'I love you,' I answered.

It was the first time we had spoken these words to each other, the morning of my fiftieth birthday.

When she was in her mid-seventies she fell and broke her wrist. Over the following eight years she suffered a number of seizures and strokes. Each time she recovered, diminished but alert. But now she could no longer step to either left or right. Often there would be a queue of people when I visited. Some of them she might not have met for years, but still she would pick up the threads of their lives and circumstances as if she had just met them the previous day. Coming to kiss her stooped head and to hold her withered hand, I often had a sense of being received in audience.

'Old age is terrible when you're unwell,' she confided. 'I wish I could die.'

Then she took one last 'turn'. Judy and I stayed by her bedside overnight in the hospital. At about half past six the next morning, Tuesday, 6 July 2010 – with the crows beginning to converse and to shake the dew off their wings in the big trees beyond the windows – she grew agitated. '*Flosc an bháis*' – the flurry of energy that is said to come over some people before they pass away. She asked for food and the nurse agreed. Judy mashed Liga biscuits, softened them with milk and sprinkled sugar on top. My mother ate with relish and remained lucid up to the moment of her death, quietly, that afternoon.

Later, Ena told me of a dream in which my father had appeared. He was standing in a large, old-fashioned mansion with grass growing right to the door. He looked changed.

'I've been waiting for her to meet me,' he said. 'She'll be here soon. I had to grow old while I was waiting.'

'Go to bed,' my father said. I was twelve or thirteen, and had my head buried in a book that I had recently got on loan from Loughrea library. 'Go to bed, can't you? It's nearly half one in the morning.'

'I'll go in a minute.'

He padded slowly up the stairs in his heavily darned socks and I felt a surge of triumph at having out-sat him for the first time. I stroked the soft bristles that grew on my chin and resumed my reading of the borrowed book, Bram Stoker's *Dracula*, which was full of must and foxing and old, dried-in stains. The clock ticked loud on the mantel; the whisper of my blood was audible behind my ears. Soon I heard my father's snores, deep and sonorous, billowing across the floorboards of the upstairs, trembling in wavelets down the knuckly banisters. They did finicky, unaccountable things to my heart.

I reached the part where Jonathan Harker was watching the Count crawl 'head down' along the moonlit Transylvanian castle wall and, as I leaned into the story with my back lightly touching the curtains, a loud rapping came against the windowpane. I swung round and swept the curtains back but there wasn't a soul to be seen, just the gloom of the big empty lawn and the small square of kitchen light cast on to it.

'The only monsters that would cost me a thought,' my mother said, 'are human monsters, and the only human monsters are the living. The dead can't harm anyone.'

Still we believed in the banshee wailing for those soon to die, and the pooka pissing on the ditch-side blackberries on All Souls' Night. And a drowning happened in the lake of Loughrea every seven years. Somehow the seven years seemed always to be nearly up and a drowning imminent but maybe – we began to tell ourselves – that was just an invention to keep us from the deep and the danger and the dark.

'The older ye lads get,' my father said, 'the more ye are gone wallop.'

He had compiled a list of 'worst crimes' from which he would draw a suitable one to admonish us.

'The worst crime is throwing stones.'

'The worst crime is stealing money.'

'The worst crime is acting the ape in public.'

He missed out on cowardliness, the worst of worst crimes. To be tarred 'yellow' was a grievous crime not just in the judgement of the schoolyard but in the reckoning of the entire parish. A boy deemed to be 'yellow' disgraced not just himself but his family too, for cowardice was seen as a running stain. You would go through burning furze to avoid the dread appellation. You would chase the sliotar and pull as if your life depended on it, and take the broken fingernail or the cracked knuckle or the cut across the eyebrow with a shrug and a dismissive laugh even while spilling blood or trembling in agony. You would fight older and hardier boys rather than be seen to back down. You would refuse to cry.

My father didn't slap us. Instead he advocated 'clean fun' and lectured from his list of worst crimes. Some neighbours weren't as tolerant. One evening while I was smoking cigarette butts with other lads out beyond our ring-fort – we had collected them off the floor of the dance carnival – a neighbour happened along, walking his push bike. Without warning he slapped BP hard across the face. The cigarette butt disappeared in a burst of sparks.

'Now, sirs,' the man said with a grind in his voice, 'I'll report you to your fathers.'

'My oul fella called it a civil-minded act,' one of the lads admitted later.

'That man had no business hitting anyone,' my father told me, but I still got reprimanded, and smoking was added to the list of worst crimes.

During dance carnival month BP and I would sneak in under the pleasant-smelling marquee canvas newly erected beside Owenie's shop. The feeling of being enclosed in airy space, the low-key light and the sporadic creak and flap of the canopy attracted us. We would skate the shiny, slippery dance floor or take to the wooden bandstand to play our dervish air guitars and imaginary saxophones while yet keeping one eye out for Ruly O'Kelly, a member of the carnival committee. Ruly, small and thin, seemed to spend all his spare time sniffing about for miscreant boys. On the night of the first dance Ena was allowed to go. Now she had a job in Hohner's and could pay her way. For the rest of us it was bed as usual, but that night my mother sat up late, waiting for Ena's return. It would be the first of many such watches on her children's behalf. The drum rhythms kept me awake, but when the wind blew south from the carnival, I could hear snatches of melody that stirred a sweet, melancholy ache.

'Romance isn't the only thing them dancers are chasing,' BP would whisper in my ear with a smirk on his freckled face.

'How do you mean?'

'Ah, I'm raving is only.'

But there was no doubting the excitement of the music lifting on the midnight wind before I drifted off to sleep to the sound of 'Unchained Melody', a recent hit for the Righteous Brothers being covered by a local showband.

Later during carnival month I noticed a bulky piece of canvas thrown casually behind the bandstand. I found underneath a wheelbarrow heaped full of florins and half-crowns – the takings from the previous night's dance. I showed BP and both of us broke into a jig. Then we sank our hands to the elbows in the silver granary until some coins threatened to slip overboard, and after that we did another jig.

'We'll bury it,' BP said. 'We'll find a safe hiding place.'

'But where's a good spot?'

'Mebbe Mullagh Beg.'

We wheeled the barrow carefully over the litter of ticket slips and the shoe-printed sawdust supplied by my father but as soon as we reached the road, the full weight of what we were doing hit us.

'Why does there have to be such a big amount?'

'Stealing money is the worst crime.'

Instead of turning left towards Mullagh Beg, we turned right, towards Owenie's shop. Owenie would know what to do, maybe even give each of us the fistful of coins we were so tempted to take anyway. Our hearts lightened at the thought, but just as we reached the shop not Owenie but Ruly O'Kelly came towards us.

'You are two honest men,' he says. 'I'll tell Father Keane about your great deed and Father Keane will announce it off the altar next Sunday.'

With his every eulogy and blessing our hopes of a reward receded, for Ruly – as my Uncle Mattie put it – 'would begrudge piss its steam'. BP and I bad-mouthed each other all the way home. Our only mercy was that Ruly didn't tell the priest or that, if he did, Father Keane didn't tell the parish. We fell back on smaller scams: 'lifted' apples from the Master's orchard, 'borrowed' bicycles just to move them a few hundred yards along the road, 'forgot' to pay for copybooks in the school shop. Soft drinks we 'found' in the carnival tent were a particular treat.

'Oh, the industrial school at Letterfrack,' Ruly admonished after seeing us uncap two bottles of Dwans lemonade against the top edge of the church wall. 'I hear tell that's the place where they stick thieving young buckos.'

One of our favourite time-killers was listening to the old men. They forgot about us or we grew invisible to them, and their tongues loosened. The crossroads was one of their places, or they might shelter under bushes or lean over shaky gate-railings solving the problems of the world. We tried to tune in but it proved to be riddle talk mostly, with odd bits that set our ears twitching – about a girl having to leave the parish because she was 'in trouble';

about the quare hawk with the 'dangerous tendency' up to his 'touflish' again; about the spinster 'put away' behind the walls of the 'big house to the east' so her relatives could claim her house and land.

'Windy feckers,' BP said, 'trying to be big men and with not a stiver at the back of them.'

Still, I didn't feel so certain. It reminded me of horror films on television, the really frightening ones, all shadowy and atmospheric and allowing only the briefest glimpses of the monster until near the end. As a child listening to the old men, I got an inkling of the 'monster' at large in the world, the monster whose existence owed something to us all, but the monster mostly stayed hidden.

Years later, after a Station Mass in our house, with the kitchen table raised on chairs serving as an improvised altar, everybody sat down to a meal in the parlour. The priest led the conversation and we smiled at his jokes. But after a while my mother questioned him about allegations of clerical involvement in the sexual abuse of children which had begun to break in the media. 'I feel ashamed of the Church,' she said, 'and I feel shaken in my faith.'

'Oh, of course there's the odd bad apple in every barrel,' he replied, dipping and dabbing at his plate. 'I'm sure the Church is doing its utmost—'

'Stop now, Father,' she said. 'And listen.'

She spoke her heart and her mind while most of the guests looked into their chicken and ham and tomato and stayed silent.

'Mary, he's a priest, an educated man,' a neighbouring woman said later. 'How could you argue with him? I would never dream of doing that.'

'You don't have to go to college to know what's right or wrong,' my mother said back.

Flowers opened their bright and scented secrets to the bees, the sunshine and the air. Beetles rode one on top of another. Dragonflies linked up in bockety wheels. Spiders came chest to chest after patient hours of cagey leg-signals and delicate approaches. Earthworms lay side by side, swollen and particularly angled in nuptial beds of frothy spit. Birds had clean, instant sex. Cats scratched and yowled. Foxes screeched at dead of night and we mistook their mating calls for the wailing of banshees. Dogs got stuck, comically facing in opposite directions until we bashed them apart with brooms or threw cold water over them. Cows in heat blundered through fences and trotted before us along the road to meet Tom Daly's bull. The bull would sniff and screw up his ringed nostrils before waddling towards the cow with his long pink pizzle unsheathed and dripping in anticipation.

Yet, if sex was everywhere, for the first nine or ten years of my life I didn't recognise it as sex. And as sex went on, blissfully or otherwise, each species to its own, I thought of it – if at all – in vague terms of the arrival of spring or seedtime, or as the restocking of the farm, or simply as nature's continuance.

But I never suspected that human beings might have sex because human beings weren't animals – human beings were 'Temples of the Holy Spirit', the very opposite of animals – and in any event the word 'sex' didn't arise and the facts of life came later, for boys at any rate, vaguely referenced in biology books at secondary school.

'Do you know how they got you?' BP asked me one afternoon in Fifth Class while the Master and Father Keane were busy chatting at the front of the room.

'Who do you mean?'

'Who do you s'pose I mean only your mother and your oul fella?'

'Tell me how.'

'The very same way as a calf is got when the cow gets bulled.'

'Ah BP, wash your mouth out with a dose of Jeyes Fluid,' I told him, but gradually I put one and one together – yes, the two of them did go upstairs some afternoons for 'rests' . . .

Sex, no less than love, went unmentioned. Our parents saw the struggle and hardship involved in providing for us as the truest expression of love. But the idea of saying that they loved us might have embarrassed them nearly as much as having to explain the workings of sex. At school, one or other of my friends eventually spoke the word, and soon we all took to printing it inside the covers of our copies, tracing over and over in biro as if to emphasise that not only did we know what sex was about but that we had any amount of experience of 'it'. The mention of sex always brought a whisper or a snigger, but in the summer between Fifth and Sixth Class when a boy on holiday from town gave us a peek at some black and white photos of bare-breasted women, we suddenly had nothing to say.

Sex became an embrace or a kiss on TV that reddened our faces if our parents happened to be watching. And sex had to do with 'jack-asses of men' who 'foisted themselves on their wives' according to Father Keane, his sermons raging on about 'abortion and contraception' and 'filth imported from England' – that 'pagan country whose entire population will eventually die out' – while his congregation coughed in unison in their pews and the meekest and most pious among them were heard to ask, 'Dear God, will he never shut up?'

For me, sex – or a version of it – happened all un-anticipated while I was in the Callows during a summer afternoon prior to my final year in primary school. I sat in my customary spot on a dry moot beside a large stone where colonies of lichen spread and spangled them-selves in crusts of yellow, in foliose patterns and clusters of sepulchral white. As I sat, glad to be on holidays and trying to decide whether or not I should wait for the guttural yet strangely ethereal voices of wading birds which dusk always brought, slow water trickled beside me through the 'middle' river and warm, all but noiseless breezes blew. The Callows allowed me to dream everything – my family and neighbours, the houses and haysheds at a decent distance, the far blue Aughty hills – in a kindly light.

I lay back looking at the hazy sky and imagining a future where I had a purpose approved of by the world and where brokenness was mended and fulfilment was mine. I would find kindness, for myself first and then for other people because it had to be done that way. I dreamed of writing a bestselling book about spiders, of winning a hurling All-Ireland for Galway, of becoming boxing champion of the world . . . The sound of voices, laughing and tinkling across the fields, made me sit up. Two young women stood on the edge of a shallow turlough whose sunlit glitter all but occluded them. I realised after some moments that they were undressing – with the intention, presumably, of skinny-dipping in the turlough. I gaped as they took off all their clothes and danced, splashing and shrieking, into the water. They were curvaceous and strong and I could see the big pale moons of their breasts bouncing and the dark, tantalising triangle of pubic hair each displayed as she leaped and twisted.

The sight acted on me electrically. I rolled on to my stomach and pressed against the mossy mound. I stared, and a salty tang thickened my tongue. My breath quickened and I could hear my heart thump, hear and feel it as I reached down to free the hard tight rod lengthening out of my groin. Again I pressed, watching the two women all the while, and felt the pleasure-burst happen there. Am I a man now? I wondered. I slid into the deep V of the river where I knew nobody could see me and, after washing and cleaning myself as best I could, made my way slowly home, feeling quietly ecstatic and yet somehow haunted.

I stole upstairs and stepped through my parents' bedroom window on to the flat roof of the front porch. No one would think to search for me there. I lay on my back enjoying the sensation of airiness and gazed up at the shape-shifting clouds – few and torn and fluffy white – with the sun whiskering my face and the cypress trees sighing across from me and the hills giving the impression of loping along the horizon. I thought of the two young women, how they looked and moved. Immediately my body was ready but I pushed the idea away.

I dozed until the tree-shadows creeping across the garden goose-bumped my skin. I got to my feet and went back through the open window. A small alarm clock and a porcelain figurine of a dancing girl stood on the mantel-piece above the empty fireplace, and a floppy sunhat with dust smudging its brim hung from the back of the door. My father's topcoat was thrown over the quilted bed. I went to smooth the two dents made by my parents' heads where the blue-striped bolster looked slightly discoloured but, feeling inexplicably full of tenderness, decided to leave things be. After going downstairs again and slipping quietly into the parlour, I leaned in at the broad inlay mirror of the oak cabinet and my face peeped back at me, as thin and pale and unchanged as ever.

'Guess who?' a voice said, some six or seven years later. A girl's voice, and the two hands pressed over my eyes from behind were a girl's fragranced hands, and the two hillocks pressing against my back had to be a girl's breasts. I tried to shake my head but she – whoever she was – wouldn't let me.

'Nope, wrong answer.'

I had been hanging around outside the Crystal Ballroom after a dance in Kiltormer when this stand-off happened. I was eighteen or so and hadn't spoken to any girls other than my sisters for years.

'Come on, last chance.'

'Don't know.'

She turned me around and there stood the girl I had sat beside so many evenings for two and a bit years on the bus home from secondary school. I would sit beside her or she would sit beside me and sometimes our thighs would touch – she wore black tights and a pinafore dress that might get hitched up a little – and a tingle would go through me. The two of us always looked straight ahead and we never spoke.

Now the long, fair ponytail had given way to a full-bodied hairdo and she wore denim and cotton instead of a convent-school outfit and had glittery stuff about her eyes.

'How you?' she smiled – a white-toothed, glam-puss smile. But then I saw a young man dressed in a three-piece suit edging in to reclaim her – the boyfriend – and all I could do was smile and turn away.

At primary school one humiliation for boys was to be made to sit beside a girl. There were two playgrounds with a wall between, reflecting the sexual segregation in the church – females to the left of the nave and males to the right. At secondary school the boys attended St Brendan's College and the girls were ensconced at the other end of the town in St Raphael's. Only at St Brigid's Tech did boys and girls mingle.

In my early teens a chink appeared in the deep freeze that had made strangers, even zombies, out of so many of us. Someone started a youth club at Gurtymadden. We enjoyed pop records and soft drinks, a table-soccer machine, space where boys and girls could meet and chat. After a few weeks, just when we were beginning to thaw out, a football broke the post-office window – the youth club was closed down and, as my father remarked on hearing the news, it became a case of 'Goodnight Irene, I can't dance'.

Some few years later, after moving to Dublin, I began to get over my shyness. I knew, or imagined that I knew, nearly every word in the dictionary, and yet I couldn't say the simple thing, the quick thing that might make girls click with me. I didn't have the guff and wasn't even sure that I wanted it.

But in disco land, where it was too loud for talk, you just had to move. And though I was a clumsy mover, the nightclub discos – wailing reverberations, synthesisers and steady beats – helped me get in rhythm. Besides, strobe lighting made all of us look as if we were moving in slow motion; there were blizzard effects and smoke machines and, in every venue, a many-faceted mirror ball casting psychedelic shapes and colours along the walls, floors and ceilings. With the consequence that I – for one – felt secure, hidden even as I threw shapes there at the heart of the dancing circle.

At first, when the slow set came on, I could hardly bear to be touched – a girl's fingertips on my skin brought sensations of pain even as they awakened and excited me. Several nights I half-thought the girl was interested but I let the moment slip, being too shy to ask. Until, through desperation as much as through going two or three times a week to dances, I began to get over my awkwardness. And felt, however fleetingly, the damp and dingy basement that was Halla Parnell transform into paradise one night when a dark, sensuous girl pressed her body against mine and touched my ear with her whispers, her lips and her feathery breath.

The first girl I dated gave me Wrigley's-fruit-gum kisses on a flagstone in the Garden of Remembrance. The second, a civil servant, had a warm flat and money to spend, but we seldom talked much and after two months she wrote saying it wouldn't be fair to continue – but gave no reason – and I didn't get to see her after that. The third, a trainee teacher at Carysfort College, had ash-blonde hair, the deepest blue eyes and a quavering accent that would turn to urgent whispers, amazing me all over. The love between us, managing at once to be both innocent and carnal, lasted throughout Second Year – then she got a job near her home place while I stayed on in Dublin, and though we exchanged letters during the summer we fell apart owing to the distance between.

By the time I had qualified as a teacher I felt confident enough to frequent discos in such 'posh' places as Lord John's, the Tara Club and Zhivago's where – it was cartooned on the backs of the buses – 'love stories begin'. But if sex was supposed to be easily available, it depended – much as with my first experience in the Callows – on what you meant by sex. Girls would go so far, or they would stop me short, or I would stop myself.

Then one night there seemed no need to stop. She, a brunette – some years older than me in her mid-twenties – wearing a lacy tank top and a short red skirt with pleats, invited me on to the disco's small dance floor. She said she worked 'in the rag trade' which involved 'travelling a good deal' and now here we were and – she leaned into me even as she leaned back – I was 'different' and maybe a little young for her but she was 'wised up'. One slow set, her fast words filling my ear, and we went outside.

'It's raining,' I said.

'I know a place.'

I imagined her apartment, a quick drive through leafy suburbs, but no – she took me in through a narrow dusty door to a small dim-lit room at the side of the nightclub, past hot pipes going full blast, and, with the music caterwauling somewhere above us, she kissed me hard on the mouth and slid her fingers up under my T-shirt and lifted it off and unzipped my jeans and eased me out and around in her hands. I felt an intoxicating mix of urgency and calmness. She undressed herself – her skirt had a zip at the side – and came close to me again, slower now, pressing mumbles and kisses on to my neck, my chest and stomach, down and down and down.

'Tickling bellies,' she breathed. 'I love tickling bellies.'

Something about the words themselves or the way she said them or what she was doing made me laugh, but she kept on and I reciprocated until I grew fit to burst with pleasure and told her as much. 'I see that,' she laughed, wrapping her arms around my shoulders and lifting and twisting up to me. 'But you're just . . . going to . . . have . . . to wait.'

'You'll get used to it,' Mrs Heagney had said, meaning the stylish navy-blue fountain pen she'd bought me for my twelfth birthday. Shortly afterwards, in Kelly the Printer's shop in Loughrea, I chose a thick cream-white notebook for its absence of lines, and looked around for things worth putting into it. Though it may seem strange that I decided on the dusts of nature, maybe what grabbed me about them – apart from their familiarity – was the fact that they appeared endless.

Slowly but surely each page grew into a meticulous column of dusts, a barrel of dusts. Compiling the lists became a mental fix, a mad-hattered collation where, I can see now, the seeds of many of the poems that would come to me later were sown.

I wrote down the wet leaves stuck to the road, the husks of dead bluebottles on windowsills, and the fevered floury mould – 'farmer's lung' – that billowed when you slipped your hand under the breast of a hay-pike while pulling fodder for the cattle. I caught the swirls of autumn foliage falling thick and fast and the trees that wouldn't smother because their discards were constantly being decayed and devoured. I noted the dust that rose when my father cut a plank of timber between his angling wrists at the bandsaw, a dust so light it could sit on the air for days – a dust he breathed in so it became part of him. I put words to the timber- and sand-grit dust that broke when he worked the hurleys to a shine. And I phrased the flutter of soot down the chimney after rain, the ashes in the grate, the smoke of kindling and the sparks that flew when a poker was applied to the sods of turf. Then, during a summer drought, I stumbled over one of the dustiest dusts imaginable, the Common Earthball fungus – it unleashed a cloud of spores that sent me raving and gesticulating wildly across the headlands. Ultimately, of course, there was the dust of our human bodies which, according to BP, 'wore us out every seven years', and the black dust of Ash Wednesday smudged on our foreheads serving to remind us that we would wear out entirely in the end.

'For dust thou art, and unto dust shalt thou return.'

I didn't want to read death in Father Keane's dust

repetition or in my own, or kowtow to repentance as so many people seemed anxious to do. I preferred to think of dust as transformative, as clay waiting to be rained on, to be shot through with light, full of potential for the next thing that might happen. Or did I simply dream up such fine notions to fool myself out of the boredom of kneeling in the church or of stooping to my dustman chores?

I received the gift of the fountain pen about the time when Tynagh Mine was going into full production, and that may ultimately be the reason why I picked dust as my theme, for everybody was living, breathing and talking dust, the difference Tynagh Mine would make, the employment it would bring, the extra money, and indeed the pollution that might be caused by its curious and unexpected dust.

The mine had started for many people as a rumour of a 'bonanza' or 'lucky strike', but for me it started as a droning sound. It was early summer 1959 and I had just returned from school, aged six, and gone out to the overgrown cotoneaster hedge – a thing I did most evenings – where a scuffle shaking the twigs or a stifled buzz dusting the leaflets told me that life and death were happening, happening together, and where I felt eager to witness the mating of these two terrible innocents. I leaned in, spider-watching, and initially didn't hear the grumbling noise overhead. Suddenly two planes – I saw them more as arrowheads than as planes – boomed out of nowhere, seeming to make a beeline for me as I craned and craned my neck to catch their flight. They flew close together and, as they whooshed past, I fell backwards.

I remember the surprise of that backwards tumble at

least as well as I do the shock of the booming planes. By the time I regained my footing they had flown right across the Callows, only to turn and head towards me once more. To and fro they thundered, always choosing a slightly different flight-path.

'Are they taking photos or what?' my father asked, standing beside me now and shielding his eyes as he gazed upwards.

'They might be making a film,' I said.

They were in fact carrying sonar equipment designed to detect certain types of rock known to have ore-bearing potential. And though the mine wouldn't become operational until 1965, six years after I had first seen the planes, people began talking about mineral deposits being found at Derryfrench, near Tynagh, four miles from our house. The opencast pit, half a mile long and half a mile wide, would reach a depth of 340 feet, and in the early 1970s, after the surface ore had been cleared, a new phase commenced underground.

Of course I knew none of this at the start. The first dust that flew was clay, curious only in that such an enormous amount of it – six and a half million tons – was pushed aside and stockpiled. The term the mining company used for this topsoil was 'overburden'. Face shovels, dump trucks, bulldozers and loaders mauled and manipulated the mining site into existence in the largest earth-moving operation ever conducted in Ireland.

I was a few months past my twelfth birthday when the mine finally geared up after being officially opened by the Taoiseach Seán Lemass on 22 October 1965. Its drumming and droning went on at all hours. Each time explosives were set off I lifted my head from whatever I happened to be doing and could picture all the people in all the parishes within earshot simultaneously lifting their heads to spare a thought for the dangerous lives of the miners.

At night, Tynagh's clustered lights would glitter across the fields. Poor will-o'-the-wisp couldn't hold a candle to those high-powered, hard-energy lights. The Callows, where I still spent time, was seldom any longer a place of quietness – and yet, in common with most people, I generally forgot the noise. Dust blew across to us – grimier and less exotic than the orange-coloured Saharan dust that had reached us once – and I recall my mother's yell as she hurried to rescue her precious whites from the clothesline.

Later I would meet the lorries as I cycled to and from secondary school in St Brendan's College, Loughrea. They carried concentrates of lead and zinc from Tynagh to Galway Docks for export. The lead concentrate took the shape of a black powder while the zinc held a grey-ash colour. By this stage both had already come through a complicated process, from crusher to concentrator mill.

Each day the crusher reduced two thousand tons of rock for transport to the concentrator mill by conveyor belt. Sometimes a rock the size of a kitchen table, too large to go into the crusher, would be broken by the force of the high explosives. These resembled strings of sausages strung on top of the rock and stuck in place with mud. The fuse would lead away to a safe spot where a battery – hand-wound – would spark the detonator. The boulder would collapse into small, manageable chunks hidden under a smother of dust. All this material would be further blitzed in huge drums where steel balls weighing several tons would rotate at speed in water pumped by a 450-horsepower motor. The rocks would be rendered to the fineness of salt. The pulverising steel balls would gradually be replaced by others as they wasted away to nothing.

The concentrator, four hundred feet long and two hundred feet wide, was the largest structure ever built west of the Shannon. The crushed material would pass through flotation cells, troughs that were agitated and ventilated by the addition of air and chemicals. The dirty froth would rise and spill just as froth from boiling potatoes might overflow a pot.

Shortly after I had begun teaching in Ballyfermot, Simon decided to give the mine a try. 'I want to see it up close,' he said. 'I might as well take on the adventure of working there.'

Production was happening solely underground at this stage. He and fifteen or twenty fellow workers, all kitted out in heavy navy overalls, steel-cap wellingtons and yellow tin-hats, travelled down a steep mine-shaft. They sped along for fifteen minutes in a tractor-hauled box – which they called Wanderly Wagon after a children's TV programme – moving from brightness through to the utterly dark tunnel: they had forgotten to switch on their lights just as they would forget to turn them off after emerging to daylight again. The 'mine smell', an inimitable mix of minerals, dust and oil, met them at the bottom.

They were taken to the underground crusher, a giant

three-storey building clamorous enough to put bells in your ears, and a fine dust spun constantly in the rays of light wherever they turned. You couldn't recognise anyone without going up close to them, and the wisest policy was to stay on the move if you did see a light, in case it happened to be that of the shift boss. The tunnels where the conveyor belts moved were brightly lit. Simon helped the fitters, carrying gelignite, detonators and long-hole drill bits. If the crusher became jammed, they would drill a hole using a jackhammer and fill it with a stick of powder gelignite. A detonator – 'the cruster operator' – would set this off.

As well as mine-shafts, there were the 'straight-down tunnels', escape routes from one section to another, used also for ventilation purposes. The boom and shock of exploding gelignite, with thirty tons of rock displaced per blast, might happen every fifteen minutes. Flying splinters could follow you up the steel stairs, but worse was the sense of danger – and dread – if an explosive misfired. Skips hoisted the blasted material to the surface.

The conveyors consisted of thick, hard canvas material, and their rollers were powered by huge engines with steel pulleys positioned at junction points. Simon's main job was to check that the conveyor belt ran smoothly. Its lower part vibrated so the fragments of rock wouldn't cause it to lock or malfunction. Still, malfunctions did happen. A conveyor empty of debris meant something was wrong. The conveyor was steady, hypnotic and lethal.

'It could lull you,' Simon explained, 'the same as a slow-moving river.'

Five men – Willie Doyle, Alfie Glynn, Paddy Connolly,

Eddie Doherty and Jan Holmgran – lost their lives during the fifteen years Tynagh Mine was in operation.

The tailings pond, still awash with pollutants, would remain after the mine had closed. Various toxins, including 420 tons of cyanide, and arsenic that was 1,600 times the recommended level, leached into the ground. Dust flew on windy summer days.

'Dust can cover a multitude,' my mother said at the start of the mine, and her remark found its way into my book of dusts.

Years later, after the mine had been abandoned, I visited through the big golden gate that had served as the entrance to a munitions factory in Birmingham during World War I. The landscape looked lunar. A strange grey dust burnished my boot-caps. I found a mangled, half-buried air compressor with the words 'Mr Peabody' written on its side. All the droning was over and done with, the machines emptied of purpose, their dull will wound down. The huge administration block still remained. Documents that must have held significance at one time littered its floor. A large poster clinging to a wall in an area where the public would have had access promised the development of 'a new strain of grass, suitable for the reseeding of mine lands'. But only a scatter of shook-looking thraneens had grown to reclaim the slag-grey acres while, here and there, a few rust-water pools sparkled so gorgeously you might be fooled into thinking they were curative if you didn't know better.

Later I wrote a novel for young people about the impact of opencast mining on a community and called it *The Lost Orchard*. My eyesight became affected by the old Erikson computer screen during the three weeks I wrote, day and night, upstairs in a cold attic room. To my delight the novel won the Eilís Dillon Memorial Award but my 20/20 vision was gone and I had to wear reading glasses from that point on. A small price compared to the hardship endured by the mining men, my brother Simon included.

'One evening,' he told me, 'an old man came over as I was washing and changing after my shift and he had advice, as most old men do. You're just a young lad and this is not a pleasant place to be and there's no future in it. Go back to making the hurls. Isn't it a grand clean job? Little did he realise.'

Simon nonetheless took his advice. He missed the shenanigans for a while – a cigarette butt dropped into an overalls pocket with smoke eventually telling the burning tale – and the banter, always louder coming up from the mine than going down. He recalled the gleam of silver on the conveyor belt – a sparkle of stars – and the quick, gripping sound of the giant magnet as it latched on to steel or iron passing along. He remembered, too, the claustrophobic sensation of working underground, the hiss of oxygen escaping from pipes in the main tunnel, and the sump at the floor of one shaft, a cold and wet and eerie place where a water valve might have sprung a leak and you had no option but to face into it with the weight of the world packed above your head.

Simon took home one memento of the underground mine – a large chunk of silver rock. On my visits from Dublin I would pick it up and blow the dust off its jagged surfaces and tilt it to catch the light to best effect. And I'd hear myself asking what, if anything, I might make of it – the imagined city of my youth, the pitch-and-toss of fortune, the prized earth. I'd place it back on its workshop windowsill and this would happen for years until in the end it became mislaid, disappeared the way the mine itself was destined to go.

'How is everyone in Foxhall, where the fleas ate the beggar man?' Vincie Lyons asked, bustling towards me from the storage area at the back of his shop.

'They're good,' I said, jiggling from foot to foot to ease the pain caused by my badly fitting shoes. The pain was always there, always bearable. Sometimes I even forgot it. On this particular day, however, my toes seemed on fire. Furthermore, having reached the age of thirteen, I wanted to be taken seriously and felt in no mood for Vincie's bamboozling chat.

His fringe, trained to cover his bald pate, fell loose as he balanced a hand on the counter.

'Riddle me this,' he said, flicking the fringe back into place. 'Do you live in Foxhall Little or in Foxhall Big?'

'Foxhall Big.'

'And the other side of the village is Foxhall Little?'

I nodded.

'But it isn't a village, is it? None of it, Foxhall Big or Foxhall Little, is a village.'

'How do you mean?'

'There's only a scatter of houses here and there. Wouldn't you at least want a street and the stretch of a terrace in order to call yourself a village? Let alone a pub or two, and maybe a shop.'

'Well,' I said, scrunching my toes inside my shoes in an effort to ease the burning sensation, 'it's a townland so.'

'Which is a townland?' he persisted. 'Foxhall Big or Foxhall Little?'

'Both of them together,' I said.

'You're joking,' he said. 'And tell us before you go any further, which of the two Foxhalls is bigger?'

'Foxhall Little is bigger.'

'And Foxhall Big is smaller,' he finished carefully, eyeing me out of an intent, straight face. 'Is that a solid fact?'

'It is a fact,' I told him.

'Ah, ye are codding us up in the two Foxhalls,' he concluded. 'I declare to God, where ye lads come from words hardly make any sense at all.'

I packed the groceries, paid for them, and Vincie Lyons threw a clutch of Colleen toffees in on top. I headed past the hurling pitch and turned right at the crossroads. My shoes bit deeper as I walked the long fall. The telegraph cables hummed quietly above the roadside, carrying what Mattie called 'stories on top of sticks'. Words sifted and sorted themselves, so many peculiar playthings taking on a life of their own inside my skull: 'booby', 'featherbrain', 'steam engine', 'Bog English', 'misfit' . . .

I stood under a pole and inhaled its tarry smell. I pressed my ear against it, not so much to listen as to feel the vibration. I looked up at the looping strands of cable and imagined distances, an elsewhere in every direction, and felt my heart flop sideways.

'You'd need to smarten yourself fairly quick,' my mother said as I came in the garden path. 'Your head is here and your backside is halfway down the road.'

184

'Maybe I'd be able to walk if these bloody shoes weren't cutting the feet from under me.'

'Let me have a look,' she said, softening, and reluctantly I complied.

The toes of both feet were bunched and crooked and cut from rubbing against the tops of the shoes. My socks were stained with blood.

'How long has this been the way?' she asked. 'Why didn't you say anything before now?'

I don't think I made a reply. And though my mother had me fitted for a new pair of shoes, no expense spared, my feet began to hurt again a few days later, but I didn't let on. The toes, permanently damaged, would cause me pain for the next ten years or so until the problem was finally alleviated. I did, however, work at making a better shape of myself. I played hurling with the parish minor team and later with St Brendan's College – 'under your feet, Loughrea' being the catchcry there. And I always enjoyed running barefoot in the Callows, whose soft give seemed the surest ground.

Still, though I continued to yearn for affection, I couldn't ask for it. Nor would my parents say they loved us any more than we would say we loved them. Maybe they saw this as toughening us to face the world. Love was always a practical thing – the removal of a thorn from your finger using a sewing needle out by the big flagstone where the light was strongest, the bolstering of a pillow for your head when you were ill, or the forking of a choice piece of lean meat from one of your parents' plates on to yours at dinnertime.

'Do you ever feel sad?' I asked my mother one evening.

'I do.'

'But do you ever feel sad for no reason?'

'It's not for no reason. It's part of being human.'

Her answer left me disappointed but maybe she was right. Either way the brokenness would never mend. It's with me still. It's as if I am the one egg in the gross of eggs in that leathery shopping bag we carried to Owenie's shop long ago which again and again got cracked, or that broke itself. I laugh and talk and forget it for a while. But it doesn't forget me. It returns. I rock back and forth – an infant riding the wooden horse, a boy racing the Callows on a pony's back, a young man taking the train home to find out whether his father is alive or dead. I lose myself in long walks and gaze at nature – a tree, a river, a fern; I am the same as them – we are the one energy. And I soar towards ecstasy listening to the music of Van Morrison.

As for poem-making, despite the pleasure of being so engrossed, I have long since found that this of itself won't heal the bruised or dinged unaccountable feeling that is part of my nature, no more than will the satisfaction of teaching nor any amount of acceptance or praise. Yet, at a very basic level, I rescue myself by the act of writing poems. And each time the sadness comes, I try to bless and embrace it and to wear it as lightly as I can.

Free secondary schooling up to Intermediate Certificate would be granted in an unexpected move by the Minister for Education, Donogh O'Malley, from 1969. But the previous year my mother, determined that I should receive a secondary education irrespective of the costs involved, had me enrolled in St Brendan's College, Loughrea. I travelled with her to town for new clothes, new school-bag, new textbooks, as well as for the enrolment itself. Then she carefully covered the books using a roll of pale, enamel-hard kitchen wallpaper and I penned my name and address on each, ending with 'The World, The Milky Way Galaxy, The Universe'.

I knew Loughrea for the times I had stood – with Simon and my father at the Fair Green near the West Bridge – flocking cattle or sheep in the chill breezes of February or December mornings. The lake was famed for trout fishing, crannóg islands and legends. I had walked the shore a few times, half-nervous that a wave might sweep me under. Then I might swim eternally among the waterlogged streets and chimney stacks of the original town that, according to folklore, had been swallowed long ago and which could still be seen on calm days wavering gently below the surface.

St Brendan's College was built on the edge of the lake, near the boathouse and across from a medieval moat that swung north, then east, then south to encompass the heart of the town before giving finally on to the lake once more near the cathedral and the patch of reedy ground where I had found a cockchafer beetle too big to fit inside the matchbox I thought to bring it home in.

'What will you train at, young lad?' a curmudgeonly neighbour asked. 'What are you good for now that you're a scholar?'

'Pay no heed to him,' my mother said when I told her. 'Just work at your books. You won't be asked to do a whole lot else after you get home in the evenings.'

I felt fortunate in avoiding the hard graft left out for my siblings, yet I also regarded myself as being in the ha'penny place compared to them where usefulness was concerned. Ena had just earned promotion in her job at Hohner's harmonica factory and Bridie would join her there some few years later after completing her Inter Cert. Simon had already commenced his carpentry apprenticeship and Vincent planned to do the same when he had finished his Leaving Cert.

I did, however, succeed in gaining entry to the A class at St Brendan's. Most of the students in that class were townies. Their confidence intimidated me at the start. Even nicknames served as a badge of friendship between them. They played rugby and didn't speak Bog English. Their accents sounded smoother, their movements looked slicker and their dress sense was sharper. But as the term went by, I became friendlier with them.

On wet days some of us stayed indoors during lunch break, playing 'push penny' on the desk used by the teachers. In fine weather the Fair Green became our go-to place. We played hurling there or eyed the strolling girls from the Tech who seemed at once alluring and out of reach, or amused ourselves in the public gallery of the Court House listening to cases that usually involved drunk and disorderly offences committed around the local towns or petty but entertaining disputes between farmers. Or we sneaked down to Mrs Corry's little shop on Dunkellin Street where most of us were content with sweets and a few of the hard-chaws craved loose cigarettes. Mrs Corry would sit leaning over her age-glossed counter as if snoozing, but in fact she was peeking into *Jackie* or some such girls' magazine, her thin, flab-skinned elbows raised against our pesky presence as if she wished to ward off the entire commotional world itself.

A favourite hang-out was the monument to Stoney Brennan on the West Bridge. It had become slimed by decades of rain and traffic-smoke and particularly by the dust of the fifty ten-ton lorries, each making four round trips per day, that brought lead, zinc, copper and silver from Tynagh Mine to Galway Port. None of us could have imagined, as we watched the burdened lorries pass, that nearly two million tons of ore concentrates would be exported for smelting in Germany, France and Belgium between 1965 and 1981.

Loughrea had boomed and grown beyond Stoney and his story. The Travellers in particular regarded him with fondness. Once a year they would gather for a few days to sing and drink and argue in his company. Stoney, the seventh son of a seventh son, was said to have been a great healer, but his powers couldn't save him when he was accused, during Famine times, of stealing a turnip. Often, as I gazed at his weather-worn head, I wondered what he would have made of the great exodus of mining wealth from Tynagh that now shook the very ground on which his monument stood – he who had been hanged on Gallows' Hill for what seemed no kind of theft at all.

The lecture-style format of secondary education threw me at first. Corporal punishment was dished out by a few teachers, while a few others relied on sarcasm. Most were fair-minded, however, and one whom I found particularly inspiring was Mr Toher, who treated us as grown-ups and who made the subject of history come alive.

Poetry held little interest for me in secondary school. I hated the scansion and analytical aspects demanded by the exams. Shelley drowning after leaving Leghorn in a small boat, or Wordsworth 'booming' his poems while he composed out of doors, or Coleridge cloud-watching as he lay on the 'leaded roof' of Christ's Hospital in London – these poets appealed to me more through the details I learned about their lives than through their poems. The suggestion that Coleridge had been 'haunted by spectres' as a young child, his attention-seeking and the mood swings he suffered, made me feel attached to him. The 'baits' which 'Mad Shelley' was subjected to wounded me too. I thought of myself as an underdog. I fell in love with the idea of supporting life's underdogs but couldn't quite get around to identifying them or to imagining how I might devise any tangible help.

Daydreams would float me through a classroom window, out where the white foam skimmed the lakeside stepping stones and formed spry cordons around the pebbledash walls of the boathouse. I would lean back at my desk as if levering against the water's resistance and hear the creaking twist of the oars as poor Percy Bysshe, with the poems of Keats in his pocket, tried to outrun the squall.

One evening, instead of participating in the kick-around at the fire station while waiting for the bus home, I crossed Barrack Street and went into Loughrea Cathedral. I had never heard of Celtic Revival Art or of the patronage of Edward Martyn after the cathedral was built at the turn of the twentieth century, nor indeed was I 'blessed' as my mother might have wished – but immediately I felt that I had entered an exalted and exalting element. I stood in the quietness, overwhelmed by the stained-glass light as I would be by a stupendous sunset seen from Mattie's square fort. I felt consoled.

Again and again I went back. The preconceptions I had about art – that it was highfalutin and remote – began to fade. I wondered at the glories that could be crafted out of common metal and wood and stone – scenes from the life of St Brendan, Patrick as a youth carrying a lamb and, stealing my untutored heart, Michael Healy's depictions of 'Our Lady Queen of Heaven' and Evie Hone's St Brigid giving bread to a hungry girl. I wondered but did not think to try creating anything for myself.

Then I found that Seumas O'Kelly, author of 'The Weaver's Grave', was a distant relation on my father's side of the family. O'Kelly's mother, Catherine, was one of the Fitzgeralds of Foxhall and her sister Ellen had been my father's grandmother. I asked my father if he had read any of O'Kelly's stories. No, he said, but then I found our surname in two of the stories in *Waysiders* and this brought closer the idea that it was entirely feasible for a writer to draw his or her material from the lives of local people and from everyday places and events. I would remember, and it would make a difference, but for now the knowledge that I was connected to a well-published author seemed enough.

My ability to memorise facts kept me at or near the top of the class for a year or two before I slid slowly down. Algebra became a particular bugbear.

'Deeley, get the stick.'

'Remember how you agreed that if we made a fair effort—'

'Deeley, get the stick.'

'I spent three hours at them equations last night.'

'Deeley, are you deaf? Get the stick.'

'Fuck off.'

The burly sports-coach maths teacher punched me several times in the head and threw me out of the room. Each morning afterwards he would jerk back his thumb and yelp, 'Deeley, out,' with the consequence that I received no instruction in maths during my remaining years at secondary school.

'You can study in the parlour,' my mother said, all unsuspecting of the bother I found myself in. 'It should be easier to concentrate there.'

I would gape out at the cypresses darkening beyond the west window, or through the south window to where the Callows began and the lights of Tynagh Mine bulged into brightness on the horizon, or lean my head on my arms and snooze before a combination of anxiety and guilt roused me to do my homework. Sounds of talk from the kitchen, or of the TV turned up loud, would tempt me back early to the family fold.

The Inter Cert loomed, but a few months beforehand Uncle Joe returned from America after having been away since 1957. He was handsome and black-haired, dapper in suit and tie, and everything about him, including his perfect white teeth and light American accent, said style. He sat in our kitchen with one leg angled on top of the other, a glass of whiskey in his hand and a bottle of whiskey under his chair which he would finish, with very little help from my father, by morning. He smoked almost constantly and every hour or so he would say, 'Any chance of another cup of tea, Mary?' My mother would oblige, leaving the kettle on a low boil so she could wet the tea for him as required.

His charm and droll humour won us over. He described a certain priest as a phoney, and criticised what he called 'pen-lickers and paper-pushers'. My mother even forgave him when he wondered, with respect to her beloved red roses scraping beyond the window, how she didn't get fed up looking out at those 'pain-in-the-ass bushes'. It struck me that the restless energy of America had quickened him to easy boredom. I hoped he would talk about the times he'd spent earning his living as a carpenter or 'chippy' among the thronged skyscraper cities, but he seemed more interested in talking about the neighbours of his youth. He named them all, the dead and the living, and on hearing that someone had passed away he would grow quiet for a moment or extol 'the finest person that ever walked in shoe leather' before recovering his ebullience in fresh laughter and chat.

'Hey Pat, you ever think of coming with me to America?' he asked then.

'I would. I would go in a minute.'

'No,' my mother said. 'You have your exams to do before you go anywhere.'

'I'll go anyway.'

'Maybe another time,' Joe said, but the damage was done. The moment would burn a hole in my mind, occasioning arguments that lasted long after he had gone.

I did poorly in my Inter Cert. My mother – not saying much, a sure sign she was vexed – scanned the 'Positions Vacant' section of the *Connaught Tribune*. At her insistence

I applied for a number of jobs. One interview resulted and my father trimmed my now longish hair and kitted me in new clothes and I was offered the position of trainee barman in a Galway city pub. I dragged a leather suitcase from under the bed and lifted from it my prized collection of Marvel comics and shoved them in where a furry dust clung to their glossy covers, and set about packing for the journey.

It was a rundown, spit-on-the-floor pub located near the quays. Most of its customers came from Castlegar, just outside the city, and spoke Irish. 'I paid for them drinks already, *a mhac*,' a middle-aged, cloth-capped man said to me one night with a glance at his friends around the table. '*Ó, i bhfad sular thug tú síos chu'am iad.*'

Oh, long before I brought them down to him indeed.

I went to the head barman, who said, 'These lads are here twenty years, and you're here a few weeks, so we'll let it sit. Try not to get caught the next time.'

My training consisted solely of being shown how to pull a pint. A 'Screwdriver', a 'Bloody Mary', a 'Rusty Nail' and much else besides would eventually find me out. An old man sipping his Guinness at the counter one quiet afternoon told me to look busy even if it meant polishing a spotless glass for an hour, and whatever else you do never yoke up a new barrel when the boss lady is present because she's terrified of the gas.

Each week a letter arrived from my mother and I would read it while eating my lunch on a bench in Eyre Square. I was a mere thirty-two miles away – admittedly a fair distance then – but her references to the woods where my father worked, helped full-time now by Simon, only deepened my homesickness. I'd always kept track of the various woods through incidents that had happened in them and I shuffled these incidents in my head as if they were a deck of playing cards.

Ballydoogan wood came back thanks to the lizard I had caught there while cleaning brambles from around a tree. The lizard slipped away, leaving its tail wriggling in my hand. The tail left a little smear of red where the ecstatic emerald in my mind had learned to expect a matching and reciprocal green. Coole Park returned when I remembered how Vincent – who was very young at the time – had tried to climb the exclosure wire around the old copper beech autograph tree in hopes of pen-knifing his moniker alongside the initials of W. B. Yeats, Lady Gregory, Seán O'Casey and others. Woodlawn I connected with the roar that erupted from my throat as I'd tried to warn Simon about the tree that was falling towards him. He couldn't hear me above the noise of my father's chainsaw and became completely covered by the tree, but when I scrambled over to rip the branches aside, there he was, huddling without a mark on him thanks to another tree 'intervening' on his behalf.

Usually I spent my free hour sitting on a stone beside the statue of the Irish writer and journalist Pádraic Ó Conaire. I held one-sided chats with Pádraic, puzzling why – since he presumably had experience of his father's two pubs going broke – he didn't seem to show sympathy for my struggles as a trainee barman. Pádraic kept his lips sealed and his eyes lowered. His hand stayed unmoving on the stone page and I wrote assuring my mother that everything was good and never once wondering if I would get back to school or hobnob as before with my friends around Stoney Brennan's statue.

At two in the morning, when the customers were gone and the glasses washed and the chairs placed upside-down on the tables, we used to go upstairs to tally the rolls of receipts with the takings from the tills. Not one red penny could be left unaccounted for. Then, after enjoying the tomato and scallion sandwiches that the pub owner cut in neat triangles for the staff, I'd venture down and out on to the old quayside streets where smells of sea mixed with smells of bleary enterprise.

The women were there every night, stiletto-heeled, flimsily dressed, striking leggy poses or strolling along the pavement. Sailors would stumble past, some of them bellowing and brawling, or would linger to make arrangements with the women. One night a woman lightly touched my cheek with her fingers. 'Hey boy,' she said. The sound of shattering glass when a row started always quickened my step. Past the gargantuan storage cylinders I would hurry, past the flanks of rust-hulled ships and the slop of black water that beat disinterestedly against the crate- and container-cluttered dock. And just when I allowed myself to relax, lulled by the strangeness of it all, steam vents would exhale from the backside of that small, run-down city yet to come into its tourist and culture boom, and I'd find myself hurrying again.

'Would you like to go to a dance at the Seapoint?' the lady who owned the pub asked me one evening. 'I have a friend Tony who will take you.'

Tony, aged about twenty-seven, showed up – in full Garda uniform. If he saw the startled look on my face, he never let on.

'Can you drive?' he asked breezily.

'Only a tractor.'

'Anyone who can drive a tractor can drive a car.'

So I drove, slowly, over Wolfe Tone Bridge. The moon shone above the River Corrib and I basked in Tony's friendliness. After a while he reckoned we had best switch drivers. 'Imagine,' he said, 'a Garda breaking the law.'

He dropped me at the Seapoint Ballroom and promised he would return to collect me later. Then he gave my hand a little squeeze – it must be for reassurance, I told myself. But I didn't even think of asking anyone to dance. The press of bodies, dunting shoulders and prising fingers of men seemingly desperate to get past each other, women elbowing and shoving with their handbags, all made me wish for the solitary coolness of the Callows. I went outside and gulped the mild breezes off Galway Bay and listened to the waves tumbling over themselves with a pleasing crash before rushing back, all suds and soothing sibilances.

When Tony reappeared, he had changed out of his uniform. 'Well,' he said. 'Did you shift?'

'No, I didn't bother.'

'You're better off. Women – trust me, I've first-hand experience – are ball-breakers. Come on, let's go.'

Ball-breakers? I had never heard that expression but, before I could give it much thought, a thin, far-sounding cry stopped me in my tracks. No, I told myself, I must have imagined it; but then it came again, faint and ghostly through the waves and the breeze.

'What are you raving about?' Tony said, amused yet impatient when I asked him to listen.

'It sounded like someone calling.'

'Courting couples,' he smiled, giving my hand another little squeeze. Friendship, as he had told me earlier, was his middle name.

We both waited for some moments but could hear only the huge, head-filling sounds of the sea and the wind. I wanted to stay there for ever, the mild breeze blowing all sad thoughts out of my head, the deliciousness of life a thing to be treasured.

'Hurry up, we'll be late for the Resurrection,' Tony said.

The roadside lights leaned in over our heads and the white lines slid hypnotically under us as we sped back towards the city. I felt exhilarated. I could almost believe I was the leading man's sidekick in a sensational Holly-wood action movie. Suddenly Tony swung off the road and stopped the car. The handbrake creaked and the upholstery did the same. He leaned towards me and put his hand on my knee.

'What?' I said, jerking my knee away.

'You,' he said. 'Come over nearer.'

'No.'

'I like you.'

'No!'

He grabbed me about the neck and pushed his other hand between my legs. The shock at what he was doing paralysed me for a moment before I kicked and scrambled to extricate myself. His knuckles clipped the side of my head, a sharp stinging pain, and his finger-ring snagged the corner of my mouth. I shunted my elbow into his face and pushed open the passenger door enough to flop sideways on to the road. Instantly he sped away, clipping off one of my shoes. I gathered myself, gasping and shaking, and retrieved the shoe.

Slowly I started towards the city, a walk of about twenty minutes, through the noisy haze of traffic and the panicky sensation that I was stepping along a narrow precipice. After reaching my lodgings, I washed and cleaned myself, very quietly, in the bathroom. What bothered me most was the spectacle of my scrunched-up toes against the white enamel. They had begun to bleed again.

I looked at my reflection in the mirror and my face reddened. What had I done? No use being a fool if you don't show it, smart people said. Whom could I tell? Who would believe me? I didn't tell my landlady. Nor did I tell the pub owner, so full of smiles and friendship the next day where her characteristic morning face was scowling and silent. I decided that I wouldn't tell my mother.

Unnerved, full of involuntary sighs, I went through the motions the next day – swept the pub threshold, served the early customers, dumped the slops into a bucket under the counter for the bar owner's husband to feed to his lanky greyhounds. Just about lunchtime the radio was switched on and a newsreader's voice told us that the body of a woman had been washed up near Salthill. It rooted me to the spot to think that hers must have been the drowning cries I had heard.

A few weeks later the pub let me go. Feeling hopeless, I returned home with a mumbled 'sorry' and waited to hear the music. Instead, my mother placed her arm about my shoulder, gave me a long look and said, 'Did you not eat at all? There's hardly a pick on you.'

I wanted to blurt everything out to her but stayed silent, gritting myself until the feeling grew manageable again.

Failure at exams, mess and broken promises would continue to be part of the story after my parents allowed me to return to secondary school. I was often giddy and inattentive in class. One wet morning, without provocation, a student clattered me across the face while we were saying the usual prayer at the end of a lesson in the science lab.

'Just you wait,' I said.

Immediately on our return to our regular classroom I attacked him, having to reach up as he was taller and bigger than me. I caught him with several punches, causing his nose to spout blood. He fell, banging his head against the blackboard, and I swung at him again. Fortunately a friend intervened, pinioning me from behind and dragging me back, for I had every intention of continuing the assault.

This incident frightened and sobered me. Later, when I thought it over, I thought of Tony and what had happened in Galway. I promised myself that I would never raise a fist to anybody again, and this turned out to be a promise I would keep. I settled to my schoolwork, finally gaining a few reasonable grades in my Leaving Cert. I was accepted at UCG but by now had set my heart on training as a primary teacher. And, after being invited for and attending at interview at Galway University, all I could do was wait.

'Did you get the call?' Mattie would ask each time he visited.

'Not yet anyway.'

My happy anticipations faded through September 1973. Then one Sunday morning while I slept on after pretending to my parents to be too sick to go to Mass, Mrs Heagney passed away. I joined the queue in the drizzle outside her house and moved in my turn beyond the drawn curtains and the stopped clock to say goodbye to the gift she was and to thank her once more for the fountain pen.

By October I had stopped hoping about teacher training college. My mother grew fretful and my father smiled a rueful smile. I had no use of the parlour any more. Ena and Bridie rehearsed there each night for a musical, singing 'Que Sera, Sera' after returning from tuning harmonica reeds in Hohner's factory. Vincent was attending St Brigid's Tech and Simon was a fully trained carpenter. 'What'll *you* do, what'll *you* do?' went the whine of the curmudgeonly old neighbour inside my head.

'God damn it to hell,' Mattie said at last, 'that acceptance surely got lost in the post. What harm is there in phoning and finding out?'

As a result of the phone call – it would never have happened without him – the college authorities told me I had been accepted, that their letter to me must indeed have got lost in the post, and that since the first term was already several weeks old, I should make myself available for lectures without delay.

'Bet you're sorry to be lavin' us now,' Paddy Joe Hough grinned.

'A small bit, maybe.'

'Sure, why would ya be sorry? All the pleasures a Dublin open before ya like a fairground.'

'They might be too expensive for a student.'

'They might, but won't they make fierce enjoyable lessons all the same?'

I packed my things and, grateful for the smiles on my parents' faces as much as for the jig in my heart, took the train to Dublin. One of the first things I did after arriving was to hug a lamppost. Dublin in 1973 looked dilapidated and gapped, but I perceived it as beautiful. I rambled, loving the quickness and the strangeness but taking no real notice of street names, and I kept getting lost.

The fact of arriving late in St Patrick's College exacerbated what I referred to as my 'direction deficit disorder'. I was lucky to make friends with Seán Doherty, a student from Glenflesk, who helped me find my way around the various lecture halls and schedules. Through him I soon found myself surrounded by Kerrymen – Gerard from Ballylongford, John from Tralee, Timmy from Lixnaw, Neil from Scartaglen, Donal from Listowel and Tim from Killarney.

Throughout First Year, a number of us shared accommodation in Grace Park Terrace. Our landlady, old and stooped and blue-haired, called us 'a crowd of slackers' each time we skipped lectures or drank too many pints. And though she provided good breakfasts for us, we also relied on milk and biscuits from Glynn's shop to fortify the meagre college food, and – after late nights out – feasted on burgers and chips in Greasy Johnny's further along Drumcondra Road. I still kept getting lost, but through it all trembled with a mixture of fright and delight at the thought of having 'escaped'.

Several freedoms that didn't happen for me at home seemed possible now. I attended concerts and browsed in bookshops, and soon progressed from Smithwick's to Southern Comfort and Drambuie in such pubs as Kennedy's and The Cat and Cage. But what I most wanted was to meet girls and, however fumblingly, I began to make their acquaintance at those discos in Halla Parnell on Parnell Square, where many of us students used to go. All life seemed a novelty, and when the grant allowance was consumed I swallowed my guilt and wrote home asking for more money – 'just enough to keep me going'.

There were five big dormitory houses in St Pat's and the rivalry between them in every sport, including slagging, was sharp. Second Years were called 'gents' and First Years 'hedgers'. Each hedger lived across the dormitory from his gent and could be asked to do menial chores for him – an imitation of the 'fagging' in England's public boarding schools. The hedger might be 'showered' or woken up late at night or have other pranks, known as 'rides', played on him. I avoided these, being an extern, and by the time I had moved into the campus as a gent, I was steady enough not to go blackguarding anybody.

Our biggest challenge in St Pat's was a series of teaching practices where we would visit designated primary schools around Dublin and be graded on our performance by college lecturers. Fail TP, the lads told each other, and you won't be back. There seemed no great pressure academically, however, and – particularly in Second Year after I had been given accommodation in the college itself – I often skipped lectures, preferring to 'take up my mattress' and join other students out under the sun on the campus hillside, where we traded stories and listened to rock music.

I delighted in having my own room in Clonmacnoise House, and in the quiet hollow late night after pub or disco, memories of home would flow. I jotted down images of the Callows, the sawmill and workshop. The more I shaped the images, the more I gained a sense of saving, almost of reliving, experiences. I became friends with John Chambers, a First Year student whose room was across from mine, and when he told me that he wrote poems, something clicked. That must be what I was trying to do as well.

Often the small hours found me scribbling above the lovely lit-green circle of the college campus with the tripping sounds caused by air-locks in the heating system rallying up and down as if a poltergeist were trying to warn me about my shameful waste of sleep. Eventually I would find myself 'outed' by some friends who stole into my room and rummaged among the scraps of poems and declaimed them with many a guffaw while I lay in bed, embarrassed, made to listen.

By March of Second Year, advertisements for teaching jobs were beginning to appear in the newspapers. I noticed that very few students received interviews on applying and so, rather than send a CV, I resolved to go directly to schools that had placed ads. The first one happened to be in Ballyfermot.

'Can you sing?' Brother James, the principal, asked me

gruffly as soon as I arrived. 'If you can sing, the job is yours.'

I sang 'Father and Son', by Cat Stevens, attempting both the deeper register of the older man and the son's higher voice and, after looking me up and down for some moments, Brother James told me that grit was a requirement of the job and that he thought I might have it and that I should return for the start of the new school year in July but meanwhile there was a 'wild bunch of young lads' unattended in Room 51 and would I ever go and mind them for the evening.

A year or so later, after completing my college exams and formally taking up the post in Ballyfermot, I began attending poetry workshops in the Grapevine Arts Centre in North Great George's Street. My main memory of the Grapevine is of constant cold, but the wonder is that it kept going at all. Jackie Aherne and Sandy Fitzgerald each led the workshop, having founded it with Anto Fahy. They were followed by Dermot Bolger, fervent with Finglas tales that only he could tell. Later Dermot would publish my early efforts in *Raven Introductions 1* but before that – in the Grapevine – there were shouters and whisperers, mediators of 'silent verse', walkers in circles reciting as they stepped, sybarites setting fire to the page as they offered it to the air.

A number of writers, including Philip Casey, Michael O'Loughlin, Anne Le Marquand Hartigan, John McNamee and Pat McCabe, would publish widely and become well known. Others fell away. All of us – poets and novelists finding our form, actors 'resting', and a portrait artist who pencil-sketched our faces in the gloom in the hope of earning a few shillings for food – encouraged or, if unable to encourage, at least suffered each other with as much grace as we could muster.

Together with fellow workshop participants I sold copies of *Grapevine Magazine* to passers-by on O'Connell Street. One issue caused a particular stir because its front cover carried Robert Ballagh's *Kite* – a depiction of a man flashing. Someone must have complained to the Gardaí, for the 'Flasher Kite' *Grapevine* was promptly taken from us and confiscated also from the shelves of the few bookshops that had been persuaded to stock it. The Grapevine Arts Centre itself would become influential over the following years through its increasingly diverse programmes and its recognition of the need for art spaces, particularly in far-flung suburban communities where the possibility of such centres had previously attracted little or no consideration.

Heartened by the Grapevine, I decided to visit the Arts Festival at Gorey, founded by Paul Funge. If I was foolish enough to try thumbing a lift on the Stillorgan dual carriageway, a farmer from Wexford was kind enough to stop. He had a small trailer full of fluttering hens in tow.

'Poetry,' I said when he asked a question.

'Poultry,' he enthused. 'That's what I'm involved in myself.'

I lacked the heart to correct him and he passed no remarks on the cut of me – Afro-style hair with rainbow bandana, black leather jacket, cheesecloth shirt, flared purple pants and wooden clogs, resembling more a refugee from the Cavaliers of the seventeenth century than a poultry farmer.

The trip to Gorey was just one of several odysseys I embarked on in my mad enthusiasm for poetry. The cost of having my poems printed at Clarke's of Ranelagh convinced me to buy a typewriter. It was portable but at least a stone in weight – nonetheless, during my summer holidays in England I hauled it around Piccadilly and Soho with a hazy notion of typing out poems while they occurred to me on the hoof. I thumbed to Brighton on the A23 and then to Taunton, where Coleridge had spent time. Through the cornfields and yellow-stone hamlets of Somerset and Wiltshire I wandered, the unused typewriter an increasing burden and my wooden clogs biting ever deeper into my toes. Later, in company with Donal Healy, a teacher friend, I reached the city of Bath before travelling the incline to Cheddar Gorge. I visited the hill walked by Tess of the d'Urbervilles and the Wessex of Thomas Hardy, whose gloominess I admired. At last I reached Stonehenge and sat where broken-hearted Tess had sat, and imagined her silent there beside me.

My travels didn't improve my poems, which remained thin and plain as pieces of ham cut from a bacon slicer. Still I wasn't discouraged. Sounds of traffic and night-life would rise from the street to rattle my smudged and rickety bedsit window as if demanding that the perpetual 'now' of the city, the beautiful and intricate workability of it, be gathered in, given a bite to eat and made to feel welcome. Slowly but surely the poems began to grow in subtlety and power.

I frequented poetry readings around Dublin city centre and shortly took on the low-key jobs of doorman, cash-taker and seating manager, becoming the one who said 'hello' and 'welcome' and dropped the few coins' entry fee into a biscuit box. I remember feeling grateful and slightly amazed that anybody at all would show up. But show up they always did, diehard poetry lovers, some distinguished, some quixotic, some with a foot in both categories.

'Are you a poet, too?' Eleanor Walsh asked me one night outside the hubbub of the Peppercanister Church where her husband, Thomas Kinsella, was reading and where the crowd was so big that we had to turn people away. I mumbled something about beginning to be a poet and her face seemed to turn pale as she regarded me with great earnestness. 'Oh, young man, I wish you well. But when I think of the hard life a poet must lead, when I think of Tom's journey . . .'

I was invited to join the board of Poetry Ireland by its founder, John F. Deane, and by its then Secretary, Rory Brennan. Through them I met other poets including John Ennis, Gabriel Rosenstock and the dear, departed Conleth Ellis. We conducted regular meetings in Buswells Hotel in Molesworth Street, across a table that was bare except for a very large plain pink jug – far from Keats's Grecian urn in appearance – which we did our best to talk around.

The board encouraged and promoted the work of poets through its literary journal, *Poetry Ireland Review*, and through regular newsletters and a book club. It provided them with a fair and equitable roster of readings, organised venues for those readings – previously the main venue had been the pub – and ensured that a decent fee was paid, rather than the thrown-sideways pint of porter which had hitherto nearly always been regarded as the adequate recompense of poets.

'Why would you waste your time at that kind of lark?' some people, even friends, would say with a laugh when I mentioned that I wrote poems. Others looked at me as if I was strange in the head or politely listened before changing the topic of conversation at the first opportunity. A football match, a golf shot, the price of petrol or the unreliability of politicians – anything, it seemed, was preferable to poetry talk.

This would continue to be the case. But there were as well the interested ones who kept me going. And there were the unexpected encouragers. I'm thinking of the cleaning lady in Ballyfermot library who asked me for my autograph after I'd said some poems there – I agreed on condition that she would give me hers. Or of the carpenters constructing a set in a television studio next to the one where I recited a poem in rehearsal – they came in to listen and warmly applauded at the end. Or of the small boy who stole up to me at a reading after the fancy questions had been asked and whispered in my ear, 'How do you become a poet?'

Forty years is a long time to devote to any passion, never mind the arduous and mostly failing craft of poem-making. Hundreds of poems written over thousands of nights, hundreds of poems published – but it was never about having a public career as a poet. The poems managed a thing much more crucial than that: they gave definition and meaning to my life. They helped me to save it.

The night I first met Judy hadn't promised much. A dire band, the last dance, and I noticed her just as the music was about to finally collapse, a tanned and shapely girl in cheesecloth and denim with a rich cascade of long dark hair. She offered me a cigarette but explained that she herself didn't smoke. She misread my accent and thought I was from London, but I hadn't the guile to pretend.

'You look Spanish,' I said.

'That's funny. I'm just back from Spain.'

'A holiday?'

'No, work – as an au pair.'

'Oh yeah?'

'To help pay my way through uni.'

'How do you say "I love you" in Spanish?'

'*Te quiero.*'

'*Te quiero, mujer.*'

'*Hijo de puta!*'

The dance ended and she retrieved her Afghan coat. We chatted briefly and she gave me her phone number. That was the start. After our nights out we would return, usually very late, to her parents' house in Rathgar and lose track of time in kisses and talk until finally I would run for sheer joy through the deserted streets back to my flat, feeling invincible as I surged through Kenilworth Road, along by Castlewood Avenue with the lights shimmering off the railings around Belgrave Square and creating an optical illusion so the railings themselves appeared to switch and swap and chase each other, working a further mesmerism on me as I passed.

Again and again I changed address, lugging my belongings in plastic sacks from box-room to basement. Each accommodation turned out to be as big a dive as its predecessor. At Judy's insistence I sent a handful of poems

to David Marcus, editor of 'New Irish Writing' in the *Irish
Press*. Shortly I received back from him a 'Yes' printed on
moss-green paper that set me hurrying, Saturday after
Saturday, from my latest abode on Leinster Road, through
frost glittering the pavement and bell-songs emanating
from the behatted clock tower of Rathmines Town Hall
– the celebrated 'four-faced liar' – to the nearest news-
agent's. Then the frantic rummaging through the pages of
the *Irish Press* would begin – and there the three poems
were at last, my words precisely as I had written them,
with my name in heavy ink on top.

'How much did you get for them three?' a neighbour
asked while I was visiting home.

'I got nine pounds.'

'God, but weren't they dear enough? I saw you scribing
a poem on the bark of a tree beyond in Myode wood
when you were only a young lad.'

Such a thing never had happened, but still . . . My
father drew his heavy-rimmed glasses out and read the
poems slowly and carefully from beginning to end. 'They
must take a lot of putting together,' he said, and I took it
as a compliment.

For a while, even the critics seemed fascinated. I was
invited to read in the Beckett Room in Trinity College as
'one of Ireland's leading younger poets'. Another myth,
but seductive, and then I felt the fear and elation of standing and delivering by heart.

I told my mother I intended entering for the Patrick
Kavanagh Award. She liked Kavanagh. His was probably
the only poetry she had read since her schooldays. I
submitted thirty poems, and received a merit prize as

the runner-up. It didn't console me. I knew that winning such a distinguished award as the Kavanagh might have helped to smooth my path, but the satisfaction would be in writing fully achieved poems, and for this to happen the long hard road needed to be taken.

As time went by, I found myself half-wishing – for a grief, a bereavement that might obsess and compel me literally to 'put my heart on the line' as a poet. With my father's death the half-wish came back to torment me. I knew it had nothing to do with his death and yet it seemed monstrous and made me seem monstrous to myself. Each evening after a day's teaching I returned to my bedsit and prayed and cried, the first time I had done either since I was a small child. I did this for several weeks, and felt that I was expiating something. Afterwards the grief, though it would never leave me, became more bearable, and I neither prayed nor cried any more – I began writing poems again.

But back at the beginning, before my father's death, there was only the cold bright exhilarating morning when the poems appeared on the 'New Irish Writing' page. They would look good, I decided, pasted on the wall of my bedsit. Later they provoked the annoyance of the landlord, nervous about the damage they might do to his crumbly plasterwork, and I couldn't help but smile. Other published pieces took up the spaces beside them, on that wall or afterwards on the next rented wall. They grew to form a crazy patchwork, and I left them there, recognising that the sunlight must come and go, yellowing and fading everything.

There were forty-six First Standard boys in my class-room in Ballyfermot but before long the number would rise to fifty-two. I told them my name and wrote it on the blackboard. They called me 'Master' and I said call me 'Teacher' instead. This must have reminded them of their lady teacher in the convent school for now some of them called me 'Miss' and laughed at the good of it. Eventually we settled for 'Sir', though 'Master' kept making a come-back.

Throughout the early days they would clamber from their desks without warning and gather around me, all talking at once.

'We have to make room,' I'd say, 'so everyone gets a chance to be heard.'

Being heard – or listening – didn't seem to matter all that much for they were overwhelmed with stories and questions of their own, and the act of speaking these seemed enough. The training I'd received, including teach-ing practice in places as diverse as Raheny and Ballybrack, left me feeling unprepared. I decided that my father was right: I would have to learn by doing, the best and maybe the only way.

Each evening I gathered what resource materials I could scrounge and planned the following day's lessons. In class I began to say what I meant and mean what I said. I praised – cautiously – the 'good' behaviours and tried to ignore the 'bad'. Every so often my acting the clown provoked laughter, but the ease with which we could switch back to work and the busy, whispering quietness falling again into place gave a more solid satisfaction. I rolled up my sleeves in the manner of Mick Long, a teacher I admired, and followed as closely as I could his example of unwavering enthusiasm and kindness. When things went askew, as they routinely did, I understood the frustration the Master must have felt in my old classroom at Mullagh, but my way of dealing with it was to change the subject we were engaged in or simply to whistle a tune out the window at the traffic speeding by on Ballyfermot Road before starting over.

During lunch-break I would stand with one or two other teachers looking from a top corridor while the pupils chased plastic footballs in the yard below. Soccer was the game – at that time we had the biggest playground of any school in Ireland, and the twelve hundred boys, organised in loose class groups playing at cross-purposes on vaguely defined 'pitches', needed every square metre of it. The Phoenix Park, crowned with big-canopied trees, might make for a restful background, but our eyes were constantly drawn back to the children's commotion. Occasionally boys would throw sandwiches or buns on to the flat concrete roof of the shed that ran the entire length of the yard, and seagulls would swoop and skirmish over the scraps. Or a lad would shimmy up a drainpipe on to the roof in defiance of the rules in order to retrieve a football, or explode under his heel a carton of milk which he had smuggled from the classroom, timing it to splash unfortunate passers-by.

The boys used their own lingo, somewhat at variance with the 'approved' English of their textbooks. During soccer games there would be shouts to 'lam it' or 'lorry it', 'golds' got scored and lads would accuse each other of being a 'hatcher' or a 'steamer' or, when serious disputes arose, would point and say, 'Your ma is a whore.' This sentence scarcely needed completing, for, while hardly understanding what it might mean, each child regarded it as the foulest of insults – so potent that in time the uttering of the first two words alone became enough to provoke mayhem. The two quarrelling boys would tear into each other, corralled by others forming a circle about them as had happened during my own childhood. The teacher on yard duty, usually the Head Brother, would intervene, and the hullabaloo of play would end with the rattling of a hand-bell identical to the one I had used as a Mass server in what now seemed another lifetime.

The reading, writing and spelling of Standard English was compulsory, but listening to the children gave me the idea that poem-making 'workshops' might help them with ways of managing and enjoying language which were largely uncatered for in the prescribed texts. We had a wealth of raw material to draw on since Ballyfermot was famous for its songs and folktales, its oral tradition going back to the inner-city tenements from which people moved to settle in the new suburban housing estates in the early 1950s.

Anecdotes were gathered from parents and grand-parents. Street songs, rhymes and incidents from the children's own lives became poems. Everything was 'in the now' and everything, no matter how crazy or trivial, could be written about or a word or phrase invented to hold it down. The mess of language our workshops spawned needed drafting and redrafting. We made limericks, haiku, yarns, recipes, odes, epitaphs and elegies.

'Are we poets now?'

The real intention, of course, was to show the children that their experiences mattered, and to encourage self-expression. We used a rudimentary hand-press to print the poems and gathered them into booklets, with poems by famous poets, including Keats's 'A Song about Myself', among them:

> There was a naughty boy,
> A naughty boy was he,
> He would not stop at home,
> He could not quiet be –

The biggest hurrah happened when local shops agreed to put the books up for sale. The few pounds we raised were given to local charities.

We devised poem broadsheets for the classroom walls and decided to colour them in. In an old press I found a big cardboard box stacked with plastic palettes and tubes of paint. The paints had dried to a crust. Maybe the palettes could be rescued. I lifted them out and suddenly scores of insects, metal-grey in colour, spilled and scattered in all directions.

'Silverfish,' I said to the children when we got over our surprise – further relating how these nocturnal creatures, among the oldest surviving species on Earth, had existed almost unchanged for three hundred million years and how I would sometimes see them 'swimming' about the cracked tilework of the old fireplace in my flat while I sat up late, writing poems.

'Living in their hidden little gaff,' one boy said.

There the thought struck me – if these children could

speak in their own idiom, so might I use the language of the people I had grown up among. Bog English, the Master had said – but wasn't it distinct, valid still? I turned to my birthplace, its myths and folktales, the primordial energies of its landscapes, the onset of modernity, the craft skills of my father and the rhymes and ballads of the old wandering bards which my mother knew by heart. Nature, the one constant on which we rely no matter how advanced we may imagine ourselves, underpinned all. The child's reference to the silverfishes' 'hidden little gaff' sparked me off, and when the book was done I called it *Turane: The Hidden Village*.

I was offered jobs in local schools in Galway over the years, but never considered moving back. I loved Dublin, my job as a teacher and later as principal of my school in Ballyfermot, enjoyed lively friendships with my colleagues there, savoured the quiet walks with Judy on the horseshoe of Cruagh Mountain, or along the west pier at Dún Laoghaire, or by the River Dodder late at night. Once in a while I visited the Callows; this was enough, for really it had always accompanied me. Even as it shrank to a smudgy shadow of its old wildness, I wrote about it, trying to reclaim it differently from the way determined by the world of progress.

Summer 1978 turned out warm and sunny. I had written to let my family know that I would be coming home but actually arrived a few minutes ahead of my letter. It felt strange watching my mother run her finger along the lines as she hurriedly, breathlessly mouthed the words. It reminded me of how she seemed to 'disappear' into her childhood in Killoran simply by talking about it. Or of the time when she 'forgot' I was there listening to her even as she told me about the wintry night in 1948 when my father had waited, 'with the icicles hanging off him', in hope of taking her to a dance in Killalaghton Hall while her mother insisted that she stay put until the Rosary was completed. Now here I found myself once more picking my moment to touch her elbow, claim her back.

'You stayed gone a long time this time,' she said, folding the letter again into its envelope.

'I kept meaning to—'

'You don't owe us any explanations. Your life is your own.'

She nonetheless had questions for me – about my job and the flat I was staying in and the cost of renting it – and stories to tell about the lambs being sold and the hay nearly saved and the tumble dryer waiting to be fixed.

Ena and Bridie arrived home from work, 'all the style'. They had brought wine for dinner but meanwhile we reminisced about the pet hedgehog from our childhood and the Callows leech I had kept for ages in a jam jar and the succession of pet lambs and stray tiger cats minded by Bridie and the long-lost Maypoles that stood in the very spot where now we were taking photos with only the gentle rustle of the cypress trees behind us to indicate passing time.

'Go and have a word with your father,' my mother said finally. 'You know the place where he will likely be.'

The shed door stood open but he was so engrossed in planing a hurley at the bumped and bruised workbench that he didn't notice me at first. Shavings curled up through the plane's mouth as he stretched into the stroke and broke off when he pulled back to begin his next line of approach. One shaving got stuck in the iron throat and he snagged and cleared it behind him. He kept the rhythm going, both hands immediately back on the plane, a jumble of shavings rising and thickening at his feet.

'Oh, is it yourself?' he said, seeing me at last and placing the plane on the bench before we shook hands. 'Welcome home.'

He asked the same questions that my mother had asked and then, as if resuming an old conversation, he started planing again. His coat-collar was slightly upturned and, though his face wore a familiar, engrossed look that might at any moment flower into laughter or devilment, I noted the thick-rimmed glasses, a fixture now on the hump of his nose, and the flecks of greyness mingling with the powdery dust in his hair and eyebrows.

I regretted not having kept in closer touch and then the thought passed as shavings streamed afresh from the plane and he appeared as redoubtable as ever, with the handle of the hurley jutting into his breastbone and its bas held against a raised edge of bench. Watching him in full flow was restful. Whenever a knot or blemish emerged in the wood, he readjusted his angle and with one stroke wiped it out. Every few moments he would dismiss shavings from the bench with a casual sweep of his hand. Finally he tested the 'spring' of the finished hurley by bending it almost double.

'There should be good lashing in that,' he said, grinning.

'Go easy,' I said. 'It would be a pity to break it.'

'No fear; it's as supple as a sally rod.'

'How many years are you at it now?'

He dandled the hurley on the air, eyeing and weighing it up. 'Oh, it must be forty years,' he said. 'Give or take.'

He pinioned the hurley between hip bone and bench and drove the plane over its heel, perfecting the curve. He thumped hard into the flat of the bas, thinning and lightening before tightening the hurley in the vice so he could smooth it with the spokeshave.

'I'm thinking of stopping,' he said. 'There are trees to cut in Ballydoogan and then . . .'

He had mentioned retirement before. Maybe he'd even meant it, but again the wood, the sawmill and the workbench would draw him back.

My brothers came in and after I'd chatted with them for a while we hauled out well-seasoned planks from the back wall and lifted them on to the bench. Vincent used a pencil to mark each along the contours of the pattern and then placed the first one on the bandsaw table for ribbing.

'You operate the control box,' Simon told me.

It was affixed to the wall, with thick cables and junction boxes and danger signs everywhere. It had a black lever for START and a red button for STOP. He leaned over the belt and tugged, giving an 'assist'. The wheels revolved. When they had gained good pace and the saw was singing its scratchy song, he raised his hand. I plunged on the black lever and pressed. Everything quickened. The motor howled before settling into a more civilised hum. At exactly the right moment I had to yank the lever up into lock position. But I misjudged. The lever stuck and the whole machine whimpered to a standstill.

I glanced at my brothers and I could feel more than see my father turning from the bench. Old inadequacies came flooding back. He drew his cap from his pocket and bashed it against the side of his leg in mock-annoyance. 'I think you're trying to blow the transformer out. There'll be no light for the neighbours tonight.'

His joke was a reference to the drain which our infamous bandsaw imposed on the local power supply. Everyone could tell when what Mick Heagney called 'the blasted contraption' was in use by the dimmed lights and flickering television screens in their front rooms. Yet nobody formally complained. My father's geniality always disarmed them. So now again as Simon leaned with his assist, I picked my moment to lock the black lever up into position.

Later I walked the Callows with my mother and the feeling of belonging rose in my bones, strong and warming as ever. I noticed that the big quagmire near the middle river had become shrunken, diffused. A neighbour had undercut it by using a dredger to drain his portion of the Callows.

'A pity,' I said, noticing how the wild flowers were thinning away to rye.

'Everything changes,' my mother said.

We looked into Keaveney's well, but its eye, cataracted with weeds, didn't blink or bubble up any more. Local people were sinking wells of their own, as my father had done, and installing electric pumps to supply their houses and farms with running water. I could hardly blame them.

Neither could I help missing the lost effervescence of the underground river which I had imagined as a water dragon with its tail emerging in the shape of the spring at Mullagh Beg and its mouth represented by Keaveney's well.

'He's thinking of giving up the job,' my mother said. 'Even so, he's still going to the wood tomorrow.'

'He told me.'

She stopped walking for a moment and looked away into the distance and then back towards me. 'Wouldn't there be great ease if he gave it all up?'

I visited my uncle and aunt's house. Mattie moved to the dresser for two glasses, into each of which he poured a generous dash of whiskey. We talked about Dublin and my life as a teacher in Ballyfermot. When I mentioned the number of children attending my class, he did a little jump of incredulity.

'Isn't it remarkable,' he said then, 'how you are able to plot and pick your way through the strange and busy streets of Dublin without ever getting lost?'

If only he knew.

I felt the whiskey sear through my gullet and listened to the crickets chirruping in the hearth as they had always done. Aunt Katie mooched around the kitchen, offering the occasional comment to no one in particular as she made tea and cut bread. Then she sat without speaking, and looked at the floor where the bucket of water stood, and smiled an enigmatic smile. Her navy-blue housecoat, flecked with tiny red and yellow flowers, made me think of the country night full of stars.

～

Next morning we drove the few miles to Ballydoogan wood. The tractor engine coughed and died reluctantly as Vincent choked off its fuel supply. We dismounted from our perches beside and behind the mudguards, stretched our legs and felt the fresh, foliage-scented air in our lungs. Brambles wrangled with our boots and everywhere ash trees stood – a tranquil crowd. My father took the heavier of the two saws, placed it on a mossy tussock and poured into separate snouts petrol and lubricating oil. 'These lads are thirsty once they get going,' he said, picking up the saw. Accompanied by Vincent, he moved a safe distance away from where Simon and I intended to work.

Soon we could hear the revving of his saw, the buzz of a hundred swarms of angry bees at first and the sporadic splutter and moan as it engaged the packed tree-flesh head on. The forester had daubed a white X at shoulder-height across the trunks of trees considered suitable for felling. Only the finest ash trees, those with stout, straight boles and wide-curving roots, would suffice for hurley making. Maybe as many as twenty trees would survive for each tree earmarked for felling.

'This one will do,' Simon said. 'You clean and I'll cut.'

I slivered off ivy from the base of the tree, working the narrow blade of my heavy-handled loy in a circle as I dug down about the roots and cleared a path for the chain-saw. I felt regretful that the most perfect trees would fall, outlived by the crooked-boled, the stunted, the immature saplings, and said as much to Simon.

'The city has made you soft,' he laughed.

Methods of tree-felling had improved, if slowly, since the laborious cross-cut used by my father in the late 1930s and early 1940s – two men sawing back and forth as low to the base of the tree as possible. A decade later he would haul down a tree by extending a steel cable out to a power take-off mounted at the rear of a tractor and then ratcheting it until the roots gave way. He also used the dangerous ploy of driving in high sixth gear after attaching a rope between tractor and tree. Occasionally, when the roots failed to snap, he would be flung on to the diesel tank and jolted through to his very marrow.

In the 1960s he and Brendan Cahalan – a tough, hard-working man not given to suffer any messing from us children and whose tractor and trailer were used to draw the timber home – swung their axes blow for blow until sweat shone on their brows and crumply white chips of root popped up, leaving the smell of fresh clay to intoxicate our nostrils.

Sometimes steel wedges were inserted where gaps had been cut, and sledgehammers used to drive the wedges deeper, eventually breaking the roots' grip.

Finally, in the 1970s, he bought his first chainsaw, a Danarm 110 Manual. Even then, the danger could scarcely be said to have lessened. Kick-back of the fast-spinning blade was a threat to the operator's body or face, and instances of a tree shifting before it was fully cut or falling in an unforeseen way increased the risk of injury or death. 'Watch the tree lean,' my father would advise, 'and make sure you have an escape.'

But now I watched Simon lean over his saw and pull the cord, lean and pull again and again. Each time the saw merely wheezed. 'Anyone would think you were shaping to hit it,' I laughed.

'I will in a minute if the damn thing don't start.'

The next moment it fumed into life, scattering dust. He cut a deep horizontal incision on one side of the tree – the direction in which he wanted it to fall. Splinters and sawdust sprayed about his boots. Smoke swirled around his squatting shape. He knelt on one knee and contemplated progress made while the spikes of the metal 'dog' fastened the saw to the tree. Then he moved to the opposite side and severed above the previous incision, a downward diagonal cut intended to link with it. Again the blade agonised. He stepped back, switching off the saw, and the branch-tops trembled. He pushed hard against the tree and I lent my weight.

'It won't budge. What's holding it?' I said.

'The hinge is holding it. It'll go soon.'

The twist of the high branches was apparent now. The tree rocked on its heels and rolled to a gap in the canopy through which it crashed, tearing and scraping. There came a bounce on its impact with the ground, a shedding of ash keys, and in the sudden stillness light poured through the newly cleared space, altering the look of everything. I restarted the saw and cut the trunk to a length of about four and a half feet.

We worked throughout the morning, moving gradually inwards. By midday we were ravenous. I lit a fire and put on the kettle. A flat-topped log served as our table.

'How's the holiday-maker?'

'Oh, looking forward to the picnic.'

'This sandwich is stale.'

'Give it to me here. If you were hungry, you'd eat it.'

'If, if. If wit was shit, the world would be a dung heap.'

The fire dwindled, small bluish flames fizzing and crawling from its blackened heart along carelessly strewn, crackly twigs. Vincent poured the dregs of the kettle over it, sending up a sizzling, dusty whoosh. Then Simon and my father started clowning, arm-wrestling across the earthed table.

'Ah, his gills are reddening,' my brother said, forcing the bigger hand down to within an inch of the grain-ringed wood. 'I have him.'

'You only think you have. I'm taking a rest, that's all. See, he still can't best the old man.'

'You're cheating. Look where your arm is, for Christ's sake.'

In the late afternoon I stole away from the terrible resonance of the chainsaws, the wrenching, groaning noise of falling timber. I crossed a stream that later would be used for floating logs from more inaccessible parts of the wood, and realised the saws were out of earshot now. Behind me ferns righted their combs, while branches I pushed through swung back into place. A grubbing creature appeared to eat the shadow it lived in, and birds looped with what I could only describe as 'exultation' through a shaft of sunlight.

I found toadstools wearing distinctive marks that put me in mind of heraldic coats-of-arms, and moss fattening between the toes of trees, and ivy climbing the crooked lattice of its bones. There were others, I knew, multitudes blending with the speckled greys and browns and greens, shunning even the meagre light or curled in damp and secret clefts.

'The thronged city of the forest,' I said to myself,

marvelling at the quietness of its strife; for strife existed here, with even the mighty trees unable to afford rest, their roots foraging underground – so many cables or pipes – vast, elaborate networks of them sending water and nutrients up to the topmost storeys where the branches angled outwards, windowing and chambering space.

Such quietness still, I could almost hear it condemning the upheaval and damage we brought. Wordsworth's 'impulse from a vernal wood' came into my head. The way we used the world, all of us, was surely a grief, but when I thought of the rough and tumble of my father's and brothers' jobs, and my own involvement, it felt disloyal as well as contradictory even to recall the old Romantic's thoughts.

Night was falling by the time I returned to the tree-felling. We hid the saws, oil drums and spades under a holly thicket and rolled tree-trunks into clearings where the tractor could carry them on its pincer-like headpiece as far as the edge of the wood. To and fro it shunted, driven by Simon, its twinned rear wheels rumbling over dives and ditches with the thick-girthed trees clenched in its mouth as if they were no heavier than matchsticks.

'Together and now' was the call we made when loading the trailer, my father lugging each tree-trunk from the deck after we'd stood it on its end and lifted. The heavier root-ends were faced towards the sides of the trailer and their handles interlocked. We balanced big logs with small so they wouldn't shift. The load narrowed gradually as it rose, each length locked inside the one it rested on. By the time we had finished, the white-faced circumferences of timber resembled shields held together in a Roman phalanx.

All four of us sat on the heap of timber still left by the roadside and talked, in no hurry to head home. This was the time of day I would come to enjoy most, the pleasant tiredness in my bones quite different from the bedraggled fatigue and collar of aches I sometimes felt after a day's teaching.

But what I especially appreciated was the chance to listen to my father. He talked about his apprenticeship as a carpenter and the satisfaction he felt even at the beginning, despite what he called the 'fierce exactness' of his boss. 'Old Killeen never hit me,' he said. 'I saw him give other lads a clout if they didn't get the measurements or the sawing done right.'

He named men he had worked with and described the fun and the arguments that would happen among them, his voice growing expansive, almost tender, under cover of the falling darkness. And he praised us for the work done and complimented me on 'managing in the city' and 'earning my living from the books'. Then, to my surprise, he asked about the poems, and whether any of them rhymed.

'They do, but not in a clear-cut way,' I said, struggling to explain.

'Wouldn't you think it would be easier to make them if they didn't rhyme?'

'Well, the rhyme might be in there, but first you have to shape the poem to say—'

'Shape it to say what you mean?'

'Yes, and as fully as you can—'

'The way you shape timber, is it? To find what's hiding underneath and bring it out with a good smart finish on it?'

'I think so. Yes.'

'I own to God,' he said with a clap of his hands, 'I must have been a poet all the time at the old bench and none of ye pretended a blessed bit about it.'

We fastened our heavy jackets and kicked the trailer tyres to see if they were holding firm enough for the journey home. Simon and I clambered on top of the load. Then, even while savouring the sweep of the headlights around each bend and the surging, swaying movement of the trailer, we kept our heads down to avoid the tractor fumes and the black branches of roadside trees floating casually towards us. The few people we met along the way cast admiring glances at the timber. It could never be mistaken for firewood.

The sharp turn through the mill-yard gate took an age to negotiate. Vincent used the hydraulic lift to tip the load with a clatter on to the sawdust. My father stood next to me after my brothers had gone indoors and the silence enveloped us. I glanced at him but he seemed lost in a world of his own, staring at the strewn logs as if their clean bulk, even their vaguely discernible annual rings, had worked some hypnotism on him. Suddenly I understood that for all his upright strength, he was growing old. This recognition brought a profound hurt.

'Not love and not money,' I heard him say quietly.

'What?' I asked, more loudly than I intended.

I waited for him to answer but he seemed not to have heard. Did he mean that nothing could compensate for the hardship of the work? Or that the environmental cost in felling timber – even if his job involved thinning rather than clear-felling ash trees and, in the case of conifers, provided for the planting of new trees to replace those he had felled – was too great?

Some gloom seemed on him, but the following morning he was reinvigorated. He had talked with my mother about continuing solely with the sawmilling and hurley-making aspects of the job, and come to settle it all in his mind. 'This wood or one more – it's near time to wind down.'

And, he said, it was time to create an up-to-date 'brander' for the hurleys. The old brand had the words 'Deeley Brothers, Sawmillers and Hurley Manufacturers, Carpentry and Joinery Works', with the address in raised type inside a rectangular box. Many years had passed since those words had been drafted, and a change was long overdue. He sketched some words on a piece of paper, inside an oval rather than a rectangular box, then placed the sketch about three-quarters of the way down the flank of a hurley. Finally he showed us what he had written, and we told him it looked good. Specifications would be sent to a brand-making company in Dublin, while changes bound up with registration, letterhead and other matters would follow on from what he called this fresh start.

Soon our family would have reason for grief. But on that quiet summery morning there was simply optimism. We could have no inkling of what was to come for, even as the boy who dreamed of the steam engine under the ground knew full well, the curious machine that exists inside everybody's head is mostly disposed to travel with any degree of accuracy only backwards.

The timber-cutting would begin again for my brothers; my mother would run the farm; my sisters would return to their jobs; and I would marry Judy and make my home with her in Dublin. But irrespective of all that the future might bring, a long time would pass before we would feel able to accept with equanimity our father's death. Still, when we did look back, it was to rejoice at having experienced moments undaunted in their open-endedness, such as that particular workshop morning when he held out a neatly scripted sign towards us suggesting the future with no full stop:

L. Deeley and Sons
Hurley Makers

'Health,' Tom Headd pronounced, each time he arrived at our house over a period of two decades from the mid-1950s to the mid-1970s, 'is cycling a bicycle.'

He, my mother's father, would pedal the two miles from Killoran to visit us each Sunday afternoon. He was bald and sallow-skinned and if all his visits seemed to merge, so did his face appear to be ready-made old and unalterable despite the passing years. He would cross his legs and clasp his hands around one knee and twiddle his thumbs while he talked, but he rigorously adhered to the guidance of his store of proverbs, including the one that told him to 'always work the dry hour'.

'We'll go for a stroll around the farm,' he would suggest to my father after they had eaten.

'We will,' my father would agree. 'But first I want to show you the new gadget I bought for the sawmill. It's a powerful labour-saver altogether.'

'We'll take a look at that on our way back,' Tom would reply, and so they would begin their circuit, the talk revolving – depending on the season – around lambing and calving, milk in big metal churns transported by lorry to the creamery in Killimor, ploughing and sowing, potatoes and potato blight, hay-saving and turf, mangels for feeding to livestock and beet for the sugar factory in Tuam . . .

'Doesn't all work start as a manual task?' my father would say after they had finally come back to his domain.

'It does surely.'

'And then doesn't some smart person build a machine to take its place?'

'They do, they do.'

'It's true of nearly any job I can think of. Whatever about a person being irreplaceable, you can be certain that with every machine there is a smarter, speedier model being invented behind it. One that's more likely to break down all the sooner, of course, in order to keep the business of machine manufacture ticking over.'

'Ah, it's hard to beat the old reliables all the same,' Tom would say, 'the scythe and the shovel and the spade.'

My father's smoothing planes would give way, a year after he died, to the swingeing, scrounging sounds of the electric planers my brothers used instead. What they did was right and sensible. For the old plane, despite its endearing and enduring good looks – mouth, iron, front and rear mahogany handles, lever cap, frog, depth adjuster and the rest – was a hardship. The electric planer could work at maybe ten times the pace and certainly with ten times less effort on the operator's part.

Even the task of driving a nail or tightening a screw largely gave way to the efficient dunt of the power tool. And then there was sandpaper, whose grit chafed and burned your fingers as it shined the hurley. My father had endured its irritations even after buying a sand belt. He had no choice for, while it was a simple matter to run the belt between the tractor pulley and that of the sawmill, he could do so only out of doors, at the mercy of the weather.

In the year before he died he became interested in the idea of setting up the sander under a dry roof, in his workshop. He loved the competence of the emery belt, whose grits were of baked aluminium oxide. He spent an entire day boring four holes, each one inch in width and several inches deep, in a thick ash block, using a breast brace. This was the frame on which he would mount the iron bearings and pulley to feed off the motor at the other end of the sand belt.

He switched on the motor and the belt worked successfully for a few moments, then wobbled and flew off. The resonance, he said, was wrong. He made refinements to the framework and tried out different pulleys but always the belt ran too fast or was otherwise unstable, flapping to left and right and eventually flying off.

Whenever he had a spare hour he would return to the sander, but he failed to make it work. What he didn't realise was that the electric-motor pulley revolved at a speed that was five times faster than the tractor pulley he had used out of doors. For ballast and balance to be correct, it required to be matched with an opposing pulley that was five times bigger in diameter than itself. Such a pulley would reduce the sand belt's speed to the appropriate rate – that generated by the tractor pulley.

'What fierce misfortune is on that sand belt anyway that it won't do what it's supposed to do?' he would say, scratching his head.

Within two weeks of his death, my brothers set about reassembling the sander and its apparatus, including framework and pulleys. Trial and error was the means to an end, and behind it all a wish to pay tribute. Pulleys of different sizes were set in motion until one was found to hold the sander to just the right pace.

When Vincent told me what they had done, I imagined my father sighing somewhere out of earshot in his spirit place, in relief as much as anything else, at the answer having been found. Maybe he smiled his endearing, slightly crooked smile which, it went without saying, we would be instantly able to recognise. The smile with which he greeted all-comers to his workshop, and which widened each time he saw Tom Headd placing his bicycle at the garden wall and walking smartly up the path. Sawmills and sheep, workshops and weanlings – the dance between the two men continued unbroken for years, my mother delighting at the delicate steps by which they closed the ground between them into true friendship. Until a time came when Tom Headd grew stiff in his bones and could no longer cycle to see us. Instead, though much less regularly on account of always being busy, my father visited him, maintaining otherwise that 'Saturday or Monday, early or late, you have to be ready to fulfil an order.'

No clock hung in the carpentry shed and no watch adorned his wrist. And yet, hard cash, despite the ceaseless striving after it, seemed secondary. Get paid what you need and let the rest of it wait – this in countermand of my mother's advice: 'Don't be a bit foolish; if you live horse, you'll eat grass.' But 'foolishness', or an excess of generosity, was ingrained in him. He hated being beholden to anybody, or of conveying the impression of needing money.

'I've a small job for you now,' farmers would say, arriving in with a broken spade or shovel. 'It'll only take a minute.'

'Small' meant uncomplicated in their eyes, but experience had taught him that 'small' often implied 'awkward' or 'protracted'. Still he nodded and smiled, holding to another of his father-in-law's adages – 'always keep the fair side out'.

Rivets, known as cup rivets or gutter bolts, were used to fix in place the stump of the spade handle. Initially he would tighten the spade on the vice before cutting the caps off the rivets with a hacksaw. Punch and lump hammer could then drive the bolts out of the wood. The stump itself was removed by means of mallet and chisel. Being tightly compacted, it would require to be eked out. A new handle was then fitted, with brace and bit used to bore holes through the 'eyes' of the spade so the new cap rivets could be inserted and driven home. The job usually took him five or six minutes where an unskilled person might take all day.

'Whatever you do, don't attempt to burn out the stump – that would play holy hell with the spade,' farmers would advise.

Eventually, as he grew tired or maybe as a pay-back for their bossiness, he would place the stump-handled spade into the dying fire last thing at night and come morning the greyed-to-ashes handle would fall away as he lifted out the implement. His customers stayed none the wiser, but the problem was in getting some of them to pay.

He unfailingly shared with us, from the bar of chocolate after a quiet pint in Muldoon's pub on Saturday nights when we were children to the twenty pounds he – and my mother – would send each fortnight to keep me in food and drink when I was a student. He asserted that a thing is only a thing and can always be replaced, and proved he meant what he said on the frequent occasions I blunted a chisel or broke a hurley or reversed a tractor into a pillar in the sawmill yard. But he often let people off without paying.

The ritual seemed to stay always the same. The farmer inspected the newly fitted handle, gripping and twisting and grunting. He dug finger and thumb in his waistcoat pocket and after an age came up with a few coppers which he tossed on to the bench, where they died a giddy death. Or he came up with nothing. 'I thought I had that money mind you now. Ah sure, won't you get it off me again.'

The sinking feeling, the twist in the gut, hurt me each time I saw this, together with the apprehension that overly generous people not only compensate for, but reward, the meanness of others. Maybe it was there my mother's insistence that we 'act practical, earn money' found its beginning. Still we always had enough because he worked hard and because she was the 'good manager' he relied on. Hurleys from ash trees, sheep troughs from cedar, fencing stakes and dressers from deal, coffins from woodchip with a veneer of beech – he knew them all, their virtues and weak spots, and he knew as well when to adjust or adapt so the orders never dried up.

But though it remained timber, timber, through strapped times and good, hurleys gave him his staple income. There were a number of patterns traditionally associated with different counties – the Kilkenny, the Cork, and Galway's own. Hurlers were fussy about how the hurley should be done up, county men especially. Everything from a comfortable grip to the weight and shape and feel of the hurley had to fit particular requirements. And yet, for all the hurls my father put through his hands, the one he cherished most was a banded and battered ancient given to him by the renowned Mullagh hurler Tony Reddin, a distant relative, who had won three All-Ireland medals playing in goal for Tipperary in the late 1940s and early 1950s.

Following Ireland's membership of the EEC in 1973 and with the introduction of more modern methods of agriculture, farmers began to earn more money. They built new houses or renovated old and he provided doors and window frames, tables, presses and chairs. Tractors and mechanisation led to a decrease in the amount of carts and handles he could sell, but now he supplied creels for trailers, grass-boards and connecting rods for finger-bar mowers, parts for binders-and-reapers and threshing mills. He even built a turntable trailer with the intention of selling it but he grew proud of it and decided to keep it for carrying timber from the wood.

Tom Headd was very old now and confined to bed. 'I always liked that man,' my father said, and promised to visit him after completing the tree-felling in Moore.

Later that evening, on hearing news of the accident, two of Tom's sons decided to visit my mother, their sister. But first they called to see Tom in what, a month later, would prove to be his deathbed.

'Are ye going somewhere?'

'No.'

'Why are ye dressed up? Did something happen?'

'Everything is grand.'

'I heard a noise earlier. It sounded like a tree falling. And then I saw this man – he was tall – standing at the foot of the bed. Is Larry Deeley all right?'

The car jittered over potholes and bumpy gravel, through the dustiness of the late summer of 2013, as we drove in along Foxhall Road towards the house where my father was born.

'It's hard to believe,' Vincent said, 'but he would be nearly a hundred now if he had lived.'

They were all gone, my father, his sisters Katie and Mary Ann, his brothers Mattie, Tommy and Joe – as well as my mother, of course – and we were becoming the new 'old people'. Beech and chestnut trees had begun to encroach on the ruined thatched cottage, and the haggard where we had helped with the gathering of Mattie's hay had turned to a grassy paddock.

I recalled the hayseed itch flaking my arms and ears and neck on those long-lost autumn evenings when we forked the hay up to my father and Jimmy Hough. The pitching was easy at the start but it would grow steep, go way over our heads. Jimmy, wiry and quick and a veteran of hayfield and racetrack, would enjoy issuing instructions to 'keep the pike straight and the middle risen' and would laugh his carefree laugh when my father ordered him back. Even now I still half-expected to see them both coming down – as if from heaven – by means of a ladder pressed against the side of the sheep-cock.

'I'll get a jug of buttermilk to take the edge off our drooth until Katie has the dinner ready,' Jimmy would say, pausing mid-step to mimic Mattie. 'Jesus, he looks like a tea-cosy,' he would say then as Mattie emerged from the house with a white handkerchief on top of his pate to ward off the sun. 'What's that you have there for us, Mattie? Is it the buttermilk?'

'No buttermilk. It's whey water, just as good.'

'Whey water, a few fistfuls of oatmeal thrown into a bucket of spring – well, don't that beat Banagher.'

One evening while we youngsters paused to gulp the grainy water, Mattie went to talk to Lex Bugler, who had just pulled in carrying yet one more tram-cock on the forklift. Lex, big and bulky enough to make the Massey Ferguson he was driving look small, stroked his Desperate Dan chin, then smiled his dazzling smile as Mattie handed him a bottle of Guinness.

'Ah, there's favour in hell,' Jimmy scowled from the height.

'That's just oil for the Massey!' Lex shouted. 'You don't

want her to sit down on us now, do you, Jimmy?'

Both men laughed, but when Lex tried to drive away again he got stuck. The back wheel scraped and spun, flinging mud and grit back over the forklift. A wodge of mud hit my knee, another splashed the side of my face. But I was too busy watching the big threaded tyre biting into the ground to take evasive action. Because for me the spinning wheel had become something else entirely, and I wanted to see exactly what it might turn up. There was a grind and a groan, a rasp and a scuffle as Lex changed gear, twisting the steering wheel in an effort to change his exit path. Even reverse didn't work. 'It's no matter now to the devil,' he said, calm as the surface of the moon, 'but we appear to be stuck.'

He dismounted, and Mattie straightened with a ruffle of his shoulders. They went to investigate but I got there first. The old gasper had exposed what seemed to be a stump of dilapidated common or garden wall.

'It's a damnable thing, Lex,' Mattie said, 'but you've uncovered the foundation of the big house.'

'What big house would that be, Mattie?' Lex asked, his voice tender, confidential.

'Ah, the big house belonging to my great-grandparents, the Fitzgeralds of Foxhall,' Mattie said in his usual grumbling throwaway voice. And suddenly so many things slotted into place in my childhood mind – the expensive cut-stone walls around Mattie's garden, the ornate pillars at either end of the large cobblestone yard, the fancy coach house, the stack of gold sovereigns handed down to Katie's possession, the ancient trees, even the names by which the fields continued to be known – Smoothing Iron,

Santa's Stocking, Square Fort, Catherine's Garden . . .

'You look as if you're miles away,' Vincent said, jolting me alert. 'Or should that be years?'

A thrush sounded his battle note as I opened with difficulty the heavy gate – it had fallen into a state of collapse – which led to Mattie's cottage, and entered the wide, perfectly pebbled yard. The clay-bricked chimney still stood – teetered it seemed – reminiscent of the head of the wicker man in a film I'd seen, and the two gables rose above the thick surrounding walls. Ivy and brambles grew within and without. The cottage windows were boarded, the doors dislocated, and a stack of blue Bangor slates leaned below a sill with spiders' webs bridging the gaps between them.

Vincent called me from across the yard. There was a grey Austin Mini Allegro and a yellow Renault 12 with a rusted boot. There was also an orange-coloured car whose make I couldn't determine, half-hidden under corrugated iron, with an ash tree root growing through its grille. And nearby a white Thompson Miniglen caravan squatted on its axle, its curtains holding the colours of a painted lady butterfly almost fully drawn across the window.

We peeped in. A bunk bed, a chair, a stove, a fire extinguisher and a car battery, a Fairy Liquid bottle resting on the draining board, and a yoghurt carton.

They might all have been awaiting Uncle Joe's return – from Toronto, New York, Philly, Chicago, Los Angeles, Fairbanks, from the many towns of his experience that were fated to remain fanciful dreams in my head. From Dublin, eventually, where he and his family settled and where he and I often met.

241

'Even after he retired,' Vincent reminded me now, 'he set up a coping lathe in his back garden in the city above. He couldn't let go of the machines and the timber.'

I moved from the cottage door to the blinded window and back, hoping to find some plaything or artefact that might have belonged to my father, but all I met was a patch of weed-ridden clay and a lone daffodil tendering a single golden bugle. There seemed no trace even of the rhubarb plants – Mattie's recurrent gift to us, which we would dip in sugar and munch as if they were candy-sticks. 'The outer leaves so big,' I wrote in a composition that got me in trouble with the older boys at school, 'one of them could float baby Moses across the Nile of our Callows.'

I thought of my father as a boy running and playing, dreaming under the thatched roof, of which not a shred remained. I still have a black and white photo of him, taken in 1928, in which he appears tall for his twelve or thirteen years. He wears shirt and tie, short trousers reaching to his knees, heavy socks and sturdy well-scuffed boots. The fingers of his right hand are placed in his corduroy jacket with only the thumb protruding. His fringe is neatly swept and a look of alert earnestness illumines his strong, thin face. Mattie, slightly taller, stands beside him, his hands clasped together and his smiling head held high.

But when did my father start falling in love with machines? Probably as a child, the same as my brothers did. 'In order to understand how a machine works,' he told us once, 'you have to take it apart and put it back together, all in rotation.'

'How fast could the steam engine travel?'

'It was slow, if ever you could knock a fank out of it at all.'

'But how slow is slow?'

'Slow as a funeral.'

And, to judge by his tone of voice, just as dismal. Strange how this miserable excuse for a power source – so exasperating to him – plugged itself into my head as a madcap stimulus, a kind of consciousness, a way of colouring thought.

'People differ,' he said to me when I was older. 'They are cut out to do different things.'

And genuine obsessions – I knew he would agree – were for life. In the coach house I found a few old offcuts of timber to suggest it had served as a rudimentary workshop. And so my father's dream, and that of his brothers, must have taken practical form well before he started his apprenticeship as a carpenter. Out of the dream would come the making of a wheel for a horse's cart. Out of the wheel another wheel, then an actual cart – this took a whole month to assemble but earned ten shillings. Out of the cart a demand by farmers for more carts, and out of these the workshop and the sawmill and so many things that happened afterwards.

My father's words – 'not love and not money' – came back to me. I puzzled over them. And I remembered how some part of me half-wished for a grief after I had begun making poems – a personal tragedy that might deepen me into becoming a heartfelt poet. The thought was repellent now as it had been then; it shocked me, and I wanted to undo it again. Yes, I loved and felt swayed by the stories behind the underdog lives of so many of my favourite poets: Shelley drowned, Keats consumed by tuberculosis, Theodore Roethke divinely mad and incarcerated in St Brigid's mental hospital in Ballinasloe – not long before, when I was aged about ten, I had seen him stand drinks to my father and the other men at John Joe Broderick's pub. But, however vaguely, I had wished for a tragedy and a tragedy had come.

I absorbed the shock, grew into the grief of my father's death. I absorbed the tragedy, and started again. I chose my father's places, the woods, the sawmill, the workshop. Now, standing in the derelict yard of his childhood, I saw that the tragedy had come almost in the nature of a gift from him to me – of another life, an alternative to his. I accepted the gift that still came, and the fact of his death. I wanted his life back, but writing poems about it was as close as I could get.

I went into the orchard, whose fruit we didn't dare to steal as children because of Mattie's wicked dog, and stood under the last apple tree – a smutted survivor of the more than twenty that once grew there. It was crooked and stumpy, huddled close to the old shed wall. The ground under it was bare, while all about bluebells and nettles contested for the open space where the sunlight slanted past a stand of tall sycamore trees. 'There was a saying,' my father told us, 'that, in the time of the big house, sods of turf would be thrown in over the high wall by neighbours and in answer apples and pears would be thrown out.'

'Will we go further?' Vincent asked.

We did, along bumpy Foxhall Road, past Mick Dillon's house. 'Hell blast ye up your holes!' Mick would shout, in jest more than anger, but now a sturdy honeysuckle bush grew through his roof. A Deutz-Fahr tractor was parked beside a fork in the road, a not-so-jolly green giant, with Fleming slurry spreader yoked on to its rear and a nose-cone bonnet such as you'd expect to see on a Formula One racing car.

In past Lena Coyne's and Bowes's uninhabited cottages we drove, in past the three little corners of land known as 'Hansheen's Gardens' that were claimed by no one, and were met along the way by two young men on a dirt-track motorcycle tearing up the tired world. We came to a final fork in the road near Cahalan's old house and made an about-turn in the shadow of a telegraph pole that had no wires connecting it to anywhere and that was covered along its length with ivy. From the height we got a clear view of gas-fuelled Tynagh Power Station, about four miles distant as the crow flies. It rose out of the wasteland of the mine, gleaming silver and cylindrical in the late-evening sunlight.

We stayed until darkness had fallen, the elaborate tower deepening to blood-red – a gargantuan, resplendent Sacred Heart lamp raised towards the heavens. And who was to say it couldn't represent that as well, even as it stood as a signifier and a symbol of the ascent of the modern world, of this ever-accelerating high-tech age which would surely flummox even my father if he happened to be with us to witness it now?

Today the Callows still comes. A boy is born there and absorbs its solitude. He hears the loop and bubble of the curlew's voice drifting down to meet the bubble and loop of the floodwaters rising. He imitates the buzz and bleat of the snipe's tail feathers by blowing on a blade of grass between his fingers. He sees the fox that might have stepped out of a storybook at school strolling upright of an evening, midge-catching in his white waistcoat. He catches the tiny glints of jet planes, impossibly high and suddenly apparent, and follows their trails fuzzing and hazing the wide, supernal blue. He waits in vain in the falling darkness for will-o'-the-wisp to show. Nights when the wind leans – a solid beast – against his bedroom window and water chortles into an overbrimming barrel, he rejoices at the wastefulness of nature, the way it replenishes by spending itself. He dreams of the shallow lake that becomes a Callows, the cat-sized ancestor of Jack the pony that lives there clopping along on unshod hooves, the ferny plants growing taller than trees in the wet heat and then shrinking back again.

But because he has more than one source, one way of happening on the huge, woolly-headed monster that is nature, he dreams as well of resurrecting the steam engine in his father's sawmill. The steam engine judders and shifts, answerable to him. It becomes a burrower into the dark and deeper recesses where he is desperate to look. When he grows up, it is still there, still able to transform itself, and one rainy autumn day it materialises as Paddy Joe Hough's hackney, waiting to take him to the city. He moves towards the old, weather-worn wheels and exhaust pipes that are built into the haphazard fencing of the field beyond the sawmill, where he sees his father waving goodbye to him.

'Stay where you are,' his father says. 'You'll ruin your good clothes.'

They have worked together all summer, talked while they worked. His father waves again but he goes to shake hands with the father. He has freshly polished and shone his shoes for the city, but he ignores the mud clinging to them. The thought strikes as he plods ever closer that this powerful, everlasting old man – who can transform all kinds of cantankerous machines into humdingers, who loves the resin-smell of Scots pine, the cool arduousness of ash – has a pallor about his face that makes him appear vulnerable and other-worldly beyond his sixty-three years. Just a short few weeks later he will torment himself for not having shouted at the top of his voice, disbarring his father from ever again cutting timber. Later still he will realise that his father's weariness is the only thing he saw, no inkling of the accident soon to happen, and that the pang he felt was his own natural sadness at leaving.

'Mind yourself,' the father says softly.

'Mind yourself,' he tells the father softly back.

These are the last words that pass between them, but the boy will talk to the father for the rest of his life, and the father, though dead and gone, will talk to him.

Glossary

amadán – a male idiot or fool

ar cuairt – literally, 'on a visit'

bas – the curved end of a hurley that provides the striking surface

bockety – crooked, misaligned

crannóg – an artificial island, used in prehistoric and medieval times in Scotland and Ireland for dwelling

dinged – dented

don't that beat Banagher – usually ironic – isn't that the best thing you've ever heard?

drooth – drought, thirst

dunt – a firm blow or hit

duskus – dusk

felloes – wooden segments, cut to shape and fitted together to make the outer rim of a cartwheel

flaggard – the wild iris, in some parts of Ireland called 'flags'

flake – a punch or slap

florin – a two-shilling coin, used until 1967, roughly equivalent to 10 pence

frake – an escapade, or a wild notion

galluses – braces

gone wallop – out of control, or behaving badly

guff – nonsense

haggard – a yard where hay, straw or other farm produce was stored

hanging the sliotar out – hitting the hurling ball out from the goal area after a score or a wide

hurley – a long wooden stick with a curved end or *bas*, used in the game of hurling, which is widely believed to be the world's oldest field game, and the fastest

head beetler – a boss, especially a self-appointed one

jennet – a hybrid that is the offspring of a male horse and a female donkey

knock a fank out of it – make an impression on something

lattitats – bills

lough – a lake, in this usage 'a water puddle'

loy – a narrow spade with a single footrest

lugs – a colloquial term for the ears

messages – errands, especially of the shopping variety

moot – a type of ridge or hillock

murrain – an antiquated term for various diseases infecting cattle and other animals; its literal meaning is 'death'

naggin – in Ireland, a measure roughly equivalent to 200 millilitres

óinseach – a female idiot or fool

oxter – armpit

poll – head

quare – strange

ribbing – the process of tapering and thinning the flanks and bas of a hurley

router – a tool used, especially in cabinet-making, to hollow out a piece of wood

sally – a willow

seanchaí – a storyteller

séideán sí – the 'ghost wind'

Sétanta – the birth-name of the mythological Irish hero Cú Chulainn, who in his boyhood slew a marauding hound by driving a sliotar down its throat with his hurley

sheep-cock – a large haystack

sliotar – leather hurling ball

stiver – a former nickel coin of the Netherlands, in this usage meaning 'the smallest possible amount'

swallyhole – a sinkhole or swallow-hole

thraneen – a stem of dried grass

thurible – a metal censer suspended from a chain and used for the burning of incense during religious services

Tibb's Eve – the opening of the Christmas season, on 23 December – something of an excuse to begin the festivities two days early

touflish – mischief

turlough – a temporary or disappearing lake found mostly in limestone regions

uilleann pipes – the characteristic national bagpipe of Ireland

well wear – 'wear it well'

Acknowledgements

My heartfelt thanks to my wife Judy Carroll Deeley, my
son and daughter Alan and Genevieve, my sisters Ena
and Bridie, and my brothers Simon and Vincent, for their
help in numerous different ways in the making of this
book. I am also indebted to Tom Sheil, Michael Nolan,
Ivy Bannister, Norman Morgan, Paul O'Donnell, Ruth
Devine, Teresa Deeley, Aisling Deeley, Brigid Deeley,
Thomas Headd, Freda Dolan, Seán and Mary Kelly,
James Silas Rogers, Gerard Beirne, Adrian Moynes,
Patricia O'Connor and Daniel Balado. Special thanks
to Jonathan Williams for believing in the work, and to
Brian Langan, Eoin McHugh and everyone at Doubleday
Ireland and Transworld UK for their care and attention.